BRIGHT iDEAS

Festivals

Written by Jill Bennett and Archie Millar

Contents

Published by Scholastic Publications Ltd,
Villiers House, Clarendon Avenue,
Leamington Spa, Warwickshire CV32 5PR.

© 1988 Scholastic Publications Ltd

Reprinted 1990, 1991, 1992, 1992, 1993

Written by Jill Bennett and
Archie Millar
Edited by Jane Bishop
Sub-edited by Jane Morgan
Illustrated by Sarah Hedley

Printed in Great Britain
by Clays Ltd, St Ives plc

ISBN 0 590 70951 8

Front and back cover: designed by Sue Limb,
photographs by Martyn Chillmaid

Introduction

Festivals are joyful occasions when people celebrate publicly what they feel or believe privately. Some are rooted in the beliefs people held in early history whilst others are connected with present religious beliefs. The word 'festival' comes from the word 'feast' and many do actually involve a feast of some kind.

The festivals mentioned in this book reflect a wide variety of religions. For each festival there is a range of activities, covering all areas of the curriculum. The ideas suggested are fun to do, but it is vital that children are not exposed to just the 'lighthearted' activities and stories without being given some understanding of their deeper significance. We hope to help develop both an appreciation and understanding of some of the means through which life's significant experiences can be expressed and a sympathetic awareness of the range of religious expression.

Festivals are an ideal starting point for trying to foster an understanding and appreciation of social and ethnic groups. Through learning about festivals from different religions we can gain greater insight into the society of which we are all part and in which traditions and beliefs of groups and individuals can be respected and valued. We hope that you and your children will enjoy the activities and festivals that we have chosen.

Jill Bennett
Archie Millar

Autumn term

Chinese kite festival

The festival also called the Festival of Ascending on High occurs between the first and ninth of September because long ago Chinese meteorologists discovered that easterly winds usually prevailed in early September thus making it more ideal weather for kite flying than any other time. On the ninth day of the festival school children have a holiday from school so that they can go to fly their kites. At the end of the day everyone lets go of his or her kite and by tradition whoever finds a kite after it has fallen to the ground should burn it.

Make a kite

Age range
Six to eleven.

Group size
Individuals.

What you need
Garden cane or dowel cut to appropriate lengths, saw, PVA adhesive, tissue-paper, thin string, sponges, paint, scissors.

What to do
Slit the ends of the cane so that string can be slipped into them (younger children will need help). Saw the cane into two pieces so that one piece is slightly longer. (You may prefer to do this in advance for the youngest children.)
Cross the two strips and wrap the string tightly around the intersection. Some PVA adhesive may be added to strengthen. Slip string around the four ends of the cane,

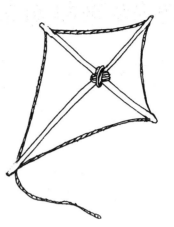

leaving one end of string hanging.
Lay the frame on tissue-paper and cut around it leaving a border. Fold the paper over the edges and stick. Cut another shape from tissue-paper and paste it to the other side so that the frame is enclosed. Cut a length of string to make a tail. Tie short lengths of tissue-paper to this string.
Assemble the kite and add string.

The tissue-paper body can be decorated with paint and sponges if the children wish. Let them try flying the kites when they are dry. They can adjust the tails by trial and error.

Ganesh's birthday

This is celebrated on the fourth day of the Hindu month Bhadrapad which usually falls in September and commemorates the birthday of Ganesh Chaturthi, the elephant-headed god of wisdom and prosperity.

Papier mâché head of Ganesh

Age range
Eight to eleven.

Group size
Individuals or pairs.

What you need
Balloons, clear petroleum jelly, newspaper, washing-up liquid bottle or similar, wallpaper paste, paint, thin card, scissors, varnish, coloured foils.

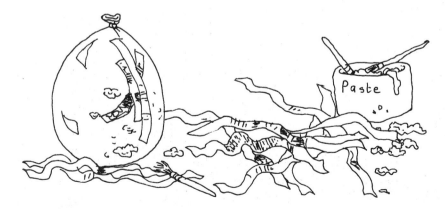

What to do
To make a basic shape, blow up the balloon and lightly coat it with clear petroleum jelly; then cover with newspaper strips soaked in wallpaper paste. At least four layers will be needed.

Hang the balloon to dry by the knot. To add the neck cut a hole (star shaped is best) in the balloon. Pull out the points and insert the washing-up liquid bottle. Fix the head into place attaching the points to the bottle with newspaper strips.

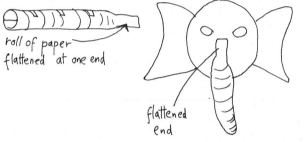

roll of paper flattened at one end

flattened end

Make a trunk by rolling paper and attaching to the head with newspaper strips. The ears can be cut from card and attached to the head in the same way.

Allow the head to dry out thoroughly, then paint it. For a final touch, add a coat of varnish. The head-dress can be cut from card, decorated and attached to the head with ordinary pins which can easily be pushed into the papier mâché.

Harvest

This is usually celebrated at around 15 October in England and Canada and is the time when Christian people give thanks to God for the harvest; the bringing in of the ripe grains, the fruit and vegetables is a cause for celebration.

In Britain when horses and carts were still used for gathering the harvest, the last cart from the fields began the harvest festival. The last sheaf of corn was twisted into the shape of a woman and placed on top of the load. This 'corn dolly' was said to embody all the elements needed for the next growing season.

Harvest is also important in many other countries: the grape harvest is an important festival in countries where wine is made, the sea harvest goes on all year round but some countries hold special harvest festivals, and the yam harvest in West Africa is another important celebration.

Cornucopia collage

Age range
Five upwards.

Group size
Individuals/whole class.

What you need
Paint, large size paper, magazines, paste and brushes, scissors.

What to do
Explain that the horn of plenty or cornucopia was a Greek mythological horn that filled itself with whatever food or drink its possessor wished.

Ask one or two children to paint a large outline shape (it would be helpful to show them pictures of a ram's horn). Ask the rest of the class or group to search through the magazines for pictures of food such as fruit, vegetables, bread and fish. The pictures can then be cut out and arranged in and around the cornucopia which is mounted on the large sheet of paper. Stick the pictures on.

Variation
This activity can also be done with words and by individuals. Each person draws a horn of plenty in the centre of the paper very lightly. The word cornucopia is then written over this thin outline as many times as is needed to cover the whole outline. The children then write the names of harvest foods coming from the mouth of the horn, thus making a word picture.

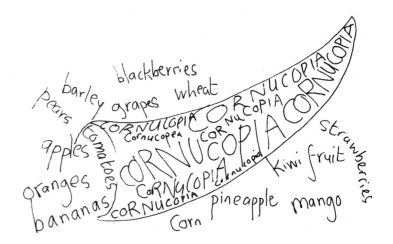

Corn dollies

Age range
Nine to eleven.

Group size
Individuals.

What you need
Drinking straws (ten per person), plastic-covered wire twists – the kind sold in packets of polythene bags (warn the children to take care of the ends), scissors.

What to do
Hold the straws together as a handful and wind the first wire twist tightly round the straws 1–2 cm from the top. This top part will represent the hair. Another twist should be tied further down about 3 cm from the first one. The area between the first and second twists will be the face.

Now pull three straws from either side of the 'body' and cut them by about one third. Bind them near the ends with twists to make the wrists.

Tie another twist roughly halfway between the neck of the doll and the bottom end of the straws to make the waist. The children can then either fan out the straws from this point to make a skirt effect or divide this section into two legs. A twist will be needed near the ends of the two sections to complete the legs.

hair

face

wrists

waist

skirt

Rosh Hashanah

Rosh Hashanah is the Jewish New Year and is celebrated on two days in September or early October. It is the beginning of the most important time of the Jewish religious year, the ten day period leading up to the Day of Atonement – Yom Kippur. The day is marked by the blowing of the shofar (ram's horn) which calls the people to prayer. At sunrise on New Year's Eve Jewish families eat a special meal.

At Rosh Hashanah it is also the custom to eat apples dipped in honey, for a fruitful new year. This could be used as the basis for a mathematical activity, each apple being cut into four quarters. Alternatively you could make honey cake.

Make a shofar

Age range
Six to eleven.

Group size
Individuals.

What you need
Newspapers, masking tape, wallpaper paste, paper towels, brown paint, scissors.

What to do
The children need to make newspaper rolls by tightly rolling one sheet and taping the ends. They will need about ten each. Ask them to curl one roll around into a circle and tape the ends together. The remaining rolls should then be taped together end to end to make one long roll. One end of the long roll is then taped to the circle and coiled around making each coil smaller than the last. Use tape to secure coils together.

Cut the paper towels into strips about 2 cm × 15 cm. In turn dip each strip into paste and lay over the newspaper coils, criss-crossing and overlapping as they go. Leave to dry completely. Paint the shofar brown.

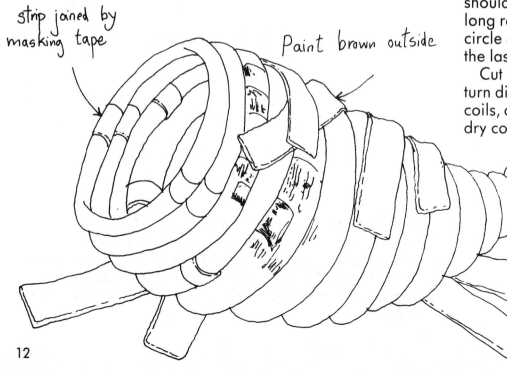

strip joined by masking tape

Paint brown outside

Honey cake

Age range
Five to eleven.

Group size
Small group.

What you need
Sieve, mixing bowl, saucepan, wooden spoon, baking tin (9 in/22.5 cm), fork or whisk.

Ingredients
375 g self-raising flour,
½ tsp allspice,
1 tsp ginger,
½ tsp bicarbonate of soda,
250 g honey,
2 eggs,
125 g sugar,
1 tbsp oil,
150 ml warm water,
20 g flaked almonds.

What to do
Pre-heat oven to 350°F/180°C/gas mark 4. Sieve flour, allspice, ginger and bicarbonate of soda together. Set to one side. Warm the honey in a saucepan over a low heat. Beat eggs and sugar till frothy and then add the honey and oil. Add one third of the flour mixture and mix well.

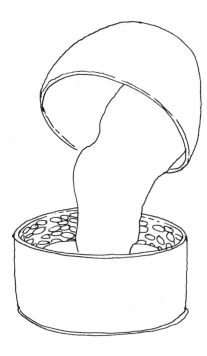

Then add half the water and mix again. Continue alternating the flour mixture and water, mixing well between each addition. Grease the baking tin and then sprinkle with almonds. Pour in the batter. Bake for approximately one hour. Remove from the tin and allow to cool.

Yom Kippur

Nine days after Rosh Hashanah is Yom Kippur, the Day of Atonement. This is the holiest day of the Jewish year and is marked by 24 hours of fasting, prayer and asking God to forgive sins. The previous evening the family gathers at sundown for a festival meal: candles are lit and members of the family ask each other for forgiveness for anything they have done wrong. After the meal everyone goes to the synagogue to pray.

The following day from early morning to sundown a service is held and at sundown the shofar is blown again to mark the closing of the gates of judgement for another year.

Forgive and forget

Age range
Six upwards.

Group size
Individuals.

What you need
Paper, pencils.

What to do
Explain to the children that at this time members of Jewish families ask each other forgiveness for wrong doings. Ask the children to think of bad or unkind things they have done to others in their family. These can be written on a list. Next ask them to decide how they will try to be better. Their ideas can be written on a separate list.

When complete the lists can be displayed around two large cut out faces – one sad and one happy.

list of unkind things

1. fight with my brother
2. told lies
3. not tidying my bedroom
4. cutting down dads geraineums
5. eating mums share of cake
6. telling Cathies secrets to someone else.

list of kind things

1. try not to fight
2. don't tell lies
3. tidy up
4. help dad in the garden
5. bake mum something
6. be nice to my best friend.

Succot

Succot or Sukkot is the Jewish feast of Tabernacles and usually occurs in September or October. It celebrates the harvest and recalls the journeys of the people of Israel through the wilderness after the Exodus from Egypt when they lived in huts.

Now sukkahs – huts or temporary dwellings made of branches and filled with fruit – are built in the synagogue and in home gardens. During the festival as many meals as possible are eaten in the sukkah and these always include harvest fruit and vegetables. The top of a sukkah is made of pine branches and fruit, vegetables and flowers are woven into the branches or hung in the hut for decoration by the children.

Model sukkah

Age range
Five to eleven.

Group size
Whole class, working in pairs.

What you need
Cardboard boxes (at least shoe-box size), scissors, adhesive, green sugar paper, crêpe or tissue-paper, coloured papers – red, yellow, orange, brown, blue.

What to do
Each pair needs a cardboard box. Ask them to cut slits in the side of the box. When this is done, turn the box so that

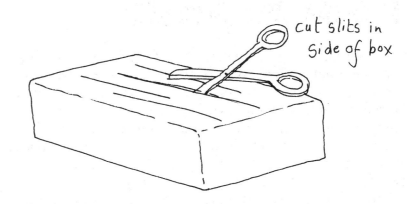

cut slits in side of box

the slit side becomes the top. Cut sprays of leaves from the green paper. Stick sprays across the top leaving spaces between so that the sky can be seen. Cut small fruits and vegetables from the coloured papers. Join them together to make 'mini' friezes. Stick one across the top of the entrance way and the others inside the sukkah.

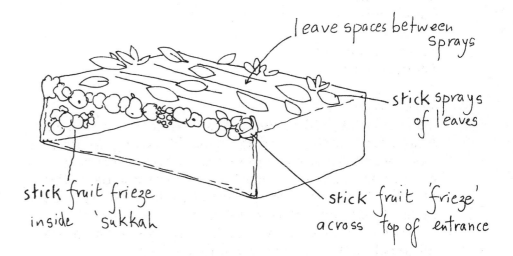

leave spaces between sprays

stick sprays of leaves

stick fruit frieze inside 'sukkah

stick fruit 'frieze' across top of entrance

Dusshera/ Ram Lila

Also called Durga Puja or Navaratri (nine nights). This Hindu festival is celebrated over ten days in September or October. It is a joint celebration of Durga and Rama. On each night different manifestations of the great warrior goddess, Mahadevi are worshipped and stories are told of her heroic or noble deeds. At the end of the festival a statue of Durga (the warrior manifestation of Devi) is lowered into a river, pool or the sea and washed.

Other celebrations include the performance of a cycle of plays – Ram Lila. Enormous models of Ravana the ten-headed demon king of Lanka are made, nine metres tall and are filled with firecrackers. A mock battle is staged (Ravana against Rama) and burning arrows are fired into the model.

During the festival, dishes of nuts and fruit curries are eaten but it is also a time for fasting. In Bengal, Dusshera coincides with the start of the harvest season and is observed as Durga Puja.

Ravana collage

Age range
Five to eleven.

Group size
Any size.

What you need
Large backing paper, small sheets of paper, paint, adhesive, pencils, coloured paper, picture or small statue of Ravana.

What to do
Draw or paint an outline of Ravana, this should be nine metres tall. Fill in the outline with paint or coloured papers. Draw or paint burning arrows on separate sheets of paper.

Next cut out the picture of Ravana and the arrows. Mount the large figure, and stick the arrows all around Ravana so that it looks as if they are being fired at him.

United Nations Day

The United Nations Organisation was established by charter on 24 October 1945. Its chief aim was to maintain international peace and security and also to develop friendly relationships and encourage co-operation internationally so that the problems facing the world could be solved.

Prayer for peace

Age range
Seven to eleven.

Group size
Individuals.

What you need
Pencils, paper.

What to do
Start by talking with the children about their feelings on peace and war in general. You might like to share with them this prayer of Dag Hammarskjöld, a former Secretary General of the United Nations, before asking them to try to write their own 'prayer for peace':

'Give me a pure heart – that I may see Thee,
A humble heart – that I may hear Thee,
A heart of love – that I may serve Thee,
A heart of faith – that I may abide in Thee.'

Hands across the world

Age range
Six to eleven.

Group size
Individuals and whole class.

What you need
Large outline map of the world, paper, pens, pencils, adhesive, atlas or globe.

What to do
Draw a large outline map of the world. (Alternatively, if the children are older you could ask a pair to do this.) Look at the globe or atlas with the children and identify the major continents and then let them suggest countries to find.

Let individuals mark these countries on the outline map. You may wish to add others depending on their list of suggestions. Display the finished map at a level the children can reach.

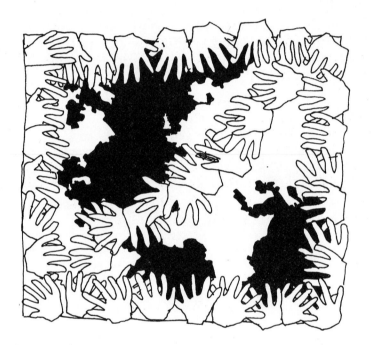

Now ask them each to draw around a partner's hands and cut these out. Each person should then glue his or her pair of cut out hands together side by side and in turn these can be stuck across the map of the world to form a chain of linked hands. Another chain of hands could also be stuck around the map to make a frame.

Lion and lamb picture

Age range
Seven to eleven.

Group size
Individuals.

What you need
Cardboard, thin card, wool – white, brown, yellow and black, PVA adhesive, scissors, pencils.

What to do
Ask the children to draw an outline of a lion on a piece of cardboard. They should then draw an outline of a lamb on another piece of card, making it much smaller than the lion. To fill in the lion shapes squeeze a line of adhesive on to a small portion of the picture and then place a strip of yellow wool on the line of adhesive.

Repeat this process working on a small area at a time until the body is completed. Fill the head in the same way and add features with black or white wool and the mane with brown.

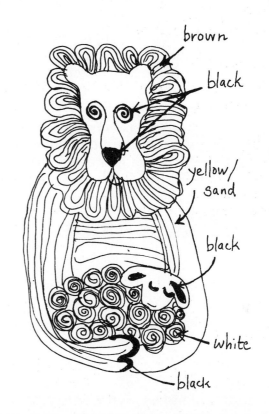

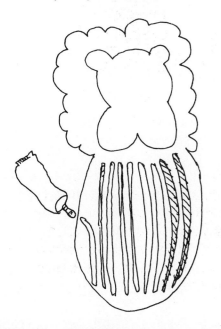

The lamb is done in a similar way with white wool, but the adhesive for the body should be squeezed out in small circle shapes and the wool twisted around over the adhesive lines to give a 'woolly' effect. Use black wool for the features. When the adhesive has dried, cut out the lamb and stick this to the body of the lion below the head and between the paws.

Diwali

Diwali is the Hindu festival of light (also celebrated by some Sikh people) and usually falls in October or November. The celebration is in honour of the return of Rama and Sita to their kingdom after 14 years in exile. It is also a celebration of light over darkness. During the feast Hindu people offer prayers to the goddess of fortune and wealth, Lakshi, and lamps – divas – are lit to welcome her into every home. The name 'Diwali' means 'a row of lights'.

The day following Diwali is New Year so this is also a time to settle disagreements and end quarrels. As part of the celebration everyone wears new clothes and cleans their house. Parties are held and presents given; people make sweets as gifts and visit relations and friends.

Indian banana fudge

Age range
Five to eleven.

Group size
Small group.

What you need
Small saucepan, rolling pin, wooden spoon, shallow tin, fork, plate, tablespoon, knife, waxed paper or pestle and mortar.

Ingredients
1 banana (as large as possible),
3 cardamom pods,
25 g margarine,
50 g semolina,
50 g ground almonds,
50 g brown sugar,
4 tbsps water.

What to do
Mash the banana with a fork and put to one side. Remove seeds from the cardamom pods and crush them between waxed paper sheets with the rolling pin or grind with a pestle and mortar if you have one. Add this to the banana. Grease the tin.

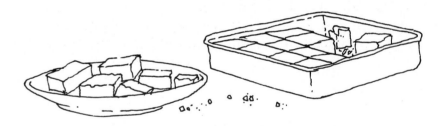

Melt the margarine in a saucepan (do not let the children do this) and gently fry the semolina until it turns golden. Stir in the banana, ground almonds, sugar and water carefully. Bring the mixture to the boil and cook slowly stirring all the time till the mixture comes away from the sides of the pan. Remove from the heat.

Spoon mixture in shallow greased tin. Place in cool place to set – if possible in a fridge. When set, cut the mixture into small squares. This should make about 12 squares; double the quantities if more are needed.

Clay divas

Age range
Five to eleven.

Group size
Individuals.

What you need
Clay in good modelling condition, acrylic based paints (optional), night lights or cotton wool and cooking oil.

What to do
Give each child a piece of clay (about an 8 cm cube). Get them to roll the clay into a ball between the palms of the hands. Press a thumb into the ball and turn between the fingers until you form a pot. Pinch one side of the pot to form a lip. Press the diva on to a hard surface to form a flat base. Make sure that the diva balances and leave to dry.

When dry it can be painted and decorated if desired. For younger children place a night light into each diva.

Older children can make a wick. Roll a small piece of cotton wool between the fingers, pinch together at one end, twisting and teasing out fibres until the wick is about 3 cm long. Pour about two teaspoons of cooking oil into the diva and float the wick. When it has soaked up some of the oil, light the twisted end. GREAT CARE is needed here – a teacher or other adult MUST supervise.

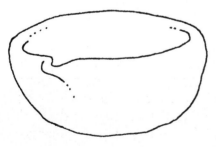

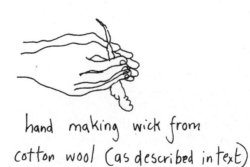

hand making wick from cotton wool (as described in text)

wick floating on cooking oil in diva.

Rangoli patterns

Age range
Five to eleven.

Group size
Individuals or pairs.

What you need
Powder paint, adhesive, adhesive brushes, large sheets of white paper, some examples of rangoli patterns if possible.

What to do
Explain to the children that Hindu people make rangoli patterns at the entrance of their homes to welcome Lakshi, the goddess of fortune and wealth, at Diwali time.

The children should draw out their patterns on the large sheets of paper. They should then decide which areas are to be in which colour. Using an adhesive brush, paint an area with adhesive, then sprinkle coloured powder paint over the adhesive. It is best to do all of one colour at the same time. Change to the next colour and repeat the process until the whole design is coloured with the paint. Leave to dry.

Diwali cards

Age range
Five to eleven.

Group size
Individuals.

What you need
Sheets of paper or thin card (A4 size approximately), paper, coloured pens, scissors, adhesive, copies of the greetings on page 119.

What to do
Asian girls celebrate festivals by decorating their hands with mehndi patterns. These make good designs for diwali cards.

Each child draws round his or her hand and colours the shape with a geometric or flower design. The hand shape is then cut out.

Fold the card in half and stick the hand shape on to the front of card. Write greeting 'Happy Diwali' inside card. (See page 119 for Diwali greetings in other languages.)

Hallowe'en

The last day of October is Hallowe'en, the eve of All Hallows' or All Saints' Day. The Celts celebrated their New Year's Eve, the Eve of Samhain, on this night. They believed that spirits were abroad so they built bonfires to frighten them away, and they danced and feasted around the fires. As well as ghosts, general mischief, witchcraft, magic and hobgoblins were anticipated.

Hallowe'en was first proclaimed as a Christian festival within the Benedictine Order in 998 and recognised in 1006 by Pope John XIX.

In America and Canada it has become a popular pastime for children to dress up and visit friends' homes to play 'Trick or treat'. This means essentially 'Give me a treat or I will play a trick on you'.

Hallowe'en mobile

Age range
Six to eleven.

Group size
Small groups (older children can work individually).

What you need
White sugar paper, black, yellow and orange paper, thread, needle or hole punch, pencils.

What to do
Draw a large crescent moon and a ghost on the white paper. Draw three small stars on the yellow paper. Draw a pumpkin on the orange paper. Draw a cat and witch on the black paper. Cut out all the shapes.

Punch (or use a needle) a small hole at the top and bottom of the moon shape. Make holes in the top of the witch, cat, ghost, pumpkin and one star. Make holes at top and bottom of two remaining stars. Thread two of the stars together. Tie thread to each of the other shapes and hang from various points around the bottom of the moon. Hang the mobile where it will move in the draughts.

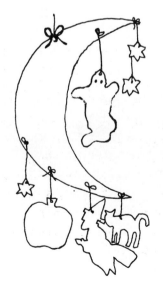

Magic writing

Age range
Five to eight.

Group size
Individuals initially, then pairs.

What you need
Kitchen paper, brushes, water paint, a selection of the following in labelled containers: adhesive, cooking oil, white wax crayons, white candles, white pencils, white chalk, white hand cream or similar.

What to do
Give each child some kitchen paper and ask them to write their names with the cooking oil. What does the paper look like now? Can they see the writing? Now tell them to paint over their pieces of paper with thin paint. What happens then? Does the name show up more now?

Let the children experiment with the other materials. Make sure they label each one. They should make two sheets from each material, one of which they paint over and one which is left unpainted. (This is to enable them to judge which marks they consider are more invisible.)

When they have had time to experiment ask the children to choose partners. They must then write invisible messages to exchange with their partners. What will they use to write with? Exchange the writing with partner. Can their partners think how to make the writing visible so they can read the messages? As it is Hallowe'en you may wish to suggest that the children write spooky messages.

Cat word games

Age range
Five to seven.

Group size
Whole class.

What you need
Stories and poems about cats, paints or pens, paper, pencils, scissors.

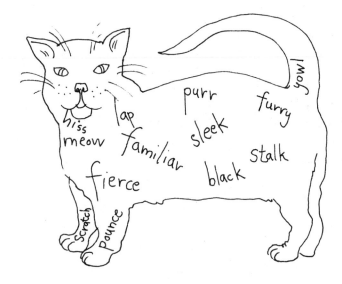

What to do
Read the children a selection of cat poems and stories over a few days. Ask one or two children to make a large cat outline using paint or pens. The children then have to think up 'catty' words to add to the picture. Each word is written, cut out and stuck on to the cat outline.

Paper bag masks

Age range
Five upwards.

Group size
Individuals.

What you need
Brown paper bags, scissors, adhesive, scraps of coloured paper/fabric, paints and brushes.

What to do
Each child needs a paper bag. Cut out holes for eyes, nose and mouth. Draw simple patterns in thick paint around the holes to exaggerate these shapes (encourage the use of a limited range of colours – eg white, black and orange for effect).

Additional detail can be added by using the scraps of materials for hair or using cut out horns, distorted ear shapes etc.

Spooky spellings

Age range
Eight to eleven.

Group size
Individuals/whole class.

What you need
A display of white ghosts with the following letters written on them: b, c, d, g, gh, h, k, l, m, n, p, t, u, w, ph, small pieces of card, pencils.

What to do
The aim is to help children become aware of the silent letters in certain spellings. They have to find words where these letters are silent. The words can be written on small pieces of card and displayed around the appropriate ghost. In the case of 'gh' it is worth pointing out which letter is pronounced, such as the 'g' in ghost.

All Souls' Day

All Souls' Day is traditionally 2 November when it was once believed that unhappy souls of the dead returned to their former homes. On All Souls' Eve kitchens were kept warm and food left on the table overnight for visiting spirits. 'Shropshire Soul Cakes' were distributed on All Souls' Day until 1850.

Belgium, The Tyrol and Bavaria also have a similar soul cake tradition.

Making soul cakes

Age range
Five to eleven.

Group size
Small groups.

What you need
Mixing bowl, sieve, wooden spoon, baking tray, teaspoon.

Ingredients
1 kg 40 g flour,
240 g butter (softened),
28 g yeast,
240 g sugar,
2 eggs,
milk for mixing,
1 tsp allspice.

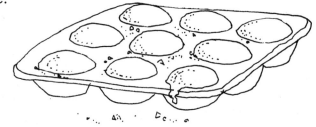

What to do
Sieve flour and work in the softened butter. Cream yeast with one teaspoon of sugar. Mix with the eggs, yeast and sufficient milk to make a light dough.

Leave the mixture in a warm place for about half an hour to rise. Then work in the sugar and allspice. Form into flat bun shapes and allow to rise for 15 minutes.

Bake at 425°F/220°C/gas mark 7 for about 15 minutes.

Guy Fawkes' Day

Bonfires are lit and effigies of Guy Fawkes made in memory of 5 November 1605 when he was discovered in the cellar of the Houses of Parliament making preparations to blow it up.

Firework code strip cartoon

Age range
Seven upwards.

Group size
Pairs or individuals.

What you need
Copy of the firework code, paper, pens or crayons.

What to do
Make sure that children know the firework code. Then ask them to produce a strip cartoon to teach younger children the code and the dangers of fireworks. It is best to suggest that they plan their ideas in rough first. (Alternatively the children could make a simple picture book for the same purpose.)

Making dummy fireworks 1

Age range
Seven to nine.

Group size
Individuals.

What you need
Copies of the nets for pyramids (see page 120), cardboard tubes, felt-tipped pens, scissors, adhesive.

What to do
First discuss the names of the various 3-D shapes with the children. They can then make dummy fireworks using the copies of the nets and cardboard cylinders. Cut out the nets and then decorate them with felt-tipped pens (this should be done before the shapes are stuck). Make sure the children make their design so that any writing will be the right way up when the shape is stuck together.

Ask the children to make up exotic names for their fireworks.

The finished shapes can be displayed against a 'fire' painting and the firework code cartoons. Alternatively a background of acrostic words built up on the word 'fireworks' could be used as a background. These words could illustrate the sights, colours, sounds and atmosphere of a firework display.

Making dummy fireworks 2

Age range
Nine to eleven.

Group size
Individuals.

What you need
Thin card, scissors, pairs of compasses, adhesive, felt-tipped pens, blue tissue-paper, ruler, pencils.

What to do
These fireworks are based on the 3-D geometric forms: the triangular pyramid, the square pyramid and the tetrahedron. Models 1 and 3 both have an equilateral triangle as the base. Draw the base in the centre of a sheet of thin card. The compass should be set at the required radius, ie the same as one of the sides of the base if making the tetrahedron and any length required if making the triangular or square pyramid. Now draw an arc with the compass point placed on one end of the corners of the base.

Repeat this process from each corner keeping the radius the same all through the exercise. Where the arcs cross each other, draw a line from that point to each of the nearest corners of the base. This gives the basic net for the model. To enable the sides to be joined, draw a flap (as shown in the diagrams) on alternate sides. Cut out the shape and fold inwards along the pencil lines.

Again any decoration should be done before the sides are glued. Glue the flaps and stick them into place so that all the edges look sharp and clean. Make small twists of blue tissue-paper to insert at the top before finally sticking the top edges together.

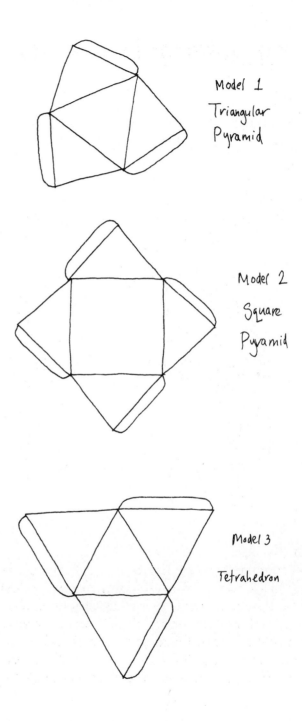

Model 1
Triangular Pyramid

Model 2
Square Pyramid

Model 3
Tetrahedron

Shichigosan

Shichigosan (Shee-CHI-goh-sahn) is the Japanese children's festival, called the Feast of Living Children. It is celebrated on 15 November and is a day of thanksgiving in honour of seven-year-old girls, five-year-old boys and all three-year-olds who have survived three 'critical periods of childhood'.

The children are presented by their parents at a shrine after which they have their photographs taken. They also receive a gift of 'candy for a thousand years'. These are long sticks of red and white candy in a bag on which are pictures of a tortoise and a crane (symbols of long life and good fortune). The children also receive balloons.

Portraits

Age range
Five to eleven.

Group size
Individuals or pairs.

What you need
Mirrors, drawing paper, crayons or chalk pastels (these are better as they can be blended).

What to do
Tell the children that on this day Japanese children have their pictures taken. Then ask them to draw self-portraits using the mirrors provided. Alternatively, the activity can be done in pairs: one of the pair draws and one sits, then swap over. The pictures could be cut out and displayed on balloon shapes.

Guru Nanak's birthday

Though he was born in April, the Sikh people celebrate the birthday of Guru Nanak in November. The festival starts two days before a full moon with a continuous reading of the Sikh holy book, the *Guru Granth Sahib*, in the Gurdwara (temple). Stories are told about the life and teaching of Guru Nanak, the founder of the Sikh faith, and the temple kitchen, Langar, offers vegetarian food to everyone. The Golden Temple in Amritsar is made even more beautiful on this special day when hundreds of tiny candles and lamps are lit. Chapatis are often served in the Sikh Langar after a service.

Golden candle decoration

Age range
Five upwards.

Group size
Individuals.

What you need
Margarine tub or similar container, thin card or cardboard tube, gold foil, adhesive, stapler, Plasticine, gold spray, coloured tissue-paper.

What to do
Cut a piece of card and roll into a cylinder (young children can use a cardboard tube), stick and staple together. Cut a flame shape from gold foil and stick to the top of candle. Put a lump of Plasticine into the margarine tub and press out. Push the candle into the Plasticine. Cut the tissue-paper flowers and stick them around the candle base. Spray the whole decoration with gold spray (make sure the surrounding area is well covered with newspaper first).

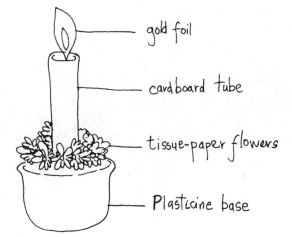

gold foil

cardboard tube

tissue-paper flowers

Plasticine base

Making chapatis

Age range
Five to eleven.

Group size
Small group.

What you need
Mixing bowl, wooden spoon, flour board, rolling pin, frying pan (heavy kind), fish slice.

Ingredients
250 g wholemeal flour,
1 tsp salt,
200 ml water,
flour for rolling,
cooking oil for frying.

What to do
Place the flour and salt in a mixing bowl and stir well. Make a well in the centre and gradually pour in water, mixing to a soft dough. Knead well for five to ten minutes. Cover the dough and leave it to stand for 30 minutes.

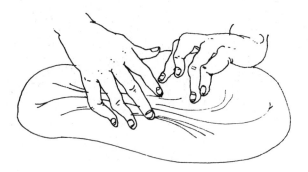

Divide the mixture among the members of the group. They should knead this again thoroughly and then cut in half. Each person then rolls out his piece of dough on a well-floured board until each is about 12 cm in diameter.

Heat a lightly oiled frying pan over moderate heat. Add the mixture and cook the chapatis until they blister (the teacher should do this). Use a fish slice to keep the chapatis from rising too much. Turn and cook the other side. Keep the chapatis hot while the others are being cooked. Serve warm.

Thanksgiving

Thanksgiving in America is celebrated on the last Thursday in November with a special dinner at which turkey is eaten in commemoration of the first Thanksgiving feast in 1621 when the Pilgrims and Indians first observed the feast.

Wax resist Thanksgiving turkey

Age range
Seven to eleven.

Group size
Individuals.

What you need
Three circle templates approximately 230 cm, 150 cm, and 40 cm in diameter (you could provide a dinner plate, a saucer and a small lid), one large sheet of white paper for each person, pencils, wax crayons, thin black paint, brushes, scissors, adhesive, one sheet of orange or yellow paper per person.

What to do
With a pencil draw a large circle in the middle of the white paper. Draw a medium-sized circle in the middle of the large circle. Draw a small circle in the middle of the medium-sized circle. Using wax crayons, draw tail feathers and feet in the large circle. Leave some spaces to be filled with black paint. Draw body feathers and

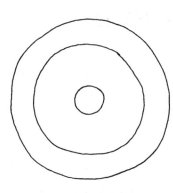

wattle in the medium-sized circle. Draw a beak, eyes and head feathers in the small circle.

Paint over the whole turkey with thin black paint. Leave to dry and then cut out the turkey shape. Discard the bottom section of the large circle. Mount on yellow or orange paper.

33

St Andrew's Day

This is celebrated on 30 November. Andrew was one of the 12 Apostles and had been a fisherman. Eventually after many travels he was imprisoned for being a Christian and condemned to death by crucifixion. Legend says that he felt he was not sufficiently worthy to die as Jesus had and requested that he should be crucified on a diagonal cross. This is now known as St Andrew's cross and is shown on the Scottish flag in white – for his purity – against a blue background representing his connection with the sea. It is said that his remains were taken to Scotland and buried where St Andrews Cathedral was subsequently built and around which the town of St Andrews developed.

Making a tartan pattern

Age range
Nine upwards.

Group size
Individuals.

What you need
A variety of coloured papers, adhesive, A4 size backing paper, rulers, pencils, scissors.

What to do
Tell the children that the various kilts and plaids are to define the clan to which the owner belongs. Ask the children to design their own. Each person will need three different coloured papers which should be cut into strips ½ cm, 1 cm and 2 cm widths.

The 2 cm strips should be stuck on to the backing paper at 1 cm intervals.

Next the 1 cm width is stuck on to the middle of the 2 cm strip running in the same direction. Finally the ½ cm strip is stuck over the other strips but running horizontally. These strips should be approximately 1 cm apart.

When finished the designs could be cut out to represent various types of clothing to be mounted on advertisements or other suitable pictures cut from magazines. The clothes could be scarves, jackets, coats, kilts or trousers.

Hanukkah

The Jewish festival of Hanukkah in December (also called the festival of lights) commemorates the victory of the Jewish people over the Syrian King, Antiochus, and the restoration of their holy temple in Jerusalem. It is said that when the temple lamp was lit it burned for eight days even though there was only enough oil to keep it alight for one day.

This is remembered today in Jewish homes when a new candle is placed in the menorah on each evening of Hanukkah until there are eight candles burning on the last evening. Hanukkah is also a special festival for children and gifts are exchanged. During this time potato pancakes called 'latkes' are also often served.

Dreidel to make

Age range
Six to eleven.

Group size
Individuals.

What you need
Thin card or white paper (A4 size), dowel, scissors, coloured pens, adhesive, copies of outline on page 121.

What to do
Explain to the children that Hanukkah is a time when people play games and in particular one called 'Spinning the Dreidel'. A dreidel is a four-sided top with Hebrew letters on each side. These represent the words 'A great miracle was there'.

Using copies of the outline on page 121 each child should cut around the outside of the net along the solid lines. Draw on the Hebrew symbols – one on each square from left to right. The symbols represent the initial letters of: Nes Gadol Hayah Sham – There was a great miracle.

| Sham | Hayan | Gadol | Nes |
| There | Was | Great | Miracle |

Fold on the dotted line so the flaps are inside and the Hebrew letters are outside. Cut or punch holes to suit the diameter of the dowel. Glue the flaps. Sharpen one end of the dowel in a pencil sharpener. When dry insert the dowel through the cube from top to bottom so the pointed end is pointing down.

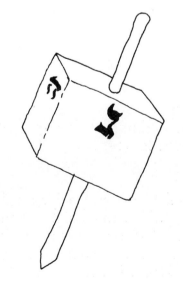

Play the dreidel game

Age range
Six to eleven.

Group size
Small group.

What you need
Dreidel, counters or sweets.

What to do
Adjust the cube up or down on the dowel until it is balanced enough to spin easily. Mark the four sides of the cube with the letters 'nun', 'gimmel', 'heh' and 'shin' in order. Each child puts in a counter or sweet to form a pool and spins the dreidel in turn to play for the pool.

If the letter 'nun' faces up the child wins nothing. If 'heh' appears, half the pool can be claimed. If 'shin' comes up, he or she must put a counter into the pool. If 'gimmel' appears, the child wins. The winner is the person who ends up with all the counters.

Make potato latkes

Age range
Five to eleven.

Group size
Small group.

What you need
Mixing bowl, grater, potato peeler (or knife), frying pan, wooden spoon, fork, teaspoon, tablespoon.

Ingredients
Several potatoes,
small onions,
1 tsp salt,
pinch of pepper,
1 tbsp flour (use matzo meal if possible),
1/2 tbsp baking powder,
2 eggs,
cooking oil for frying.

What to do
Peel the potatoes and soak in cold water. Then grate them and remove any liquid. About 2 cups of grated potato is needed. Add grated onion, salt and pepper. Mix the flour and baking powder and add to the potato mixture with the beaten eggs.

Drop spoonfuls of the mixture into a hot, well-greased frying pan and spread with the back of a spoon. When one side is brown, turn. Drain off any fat. (Potato latkes are specially good when served with apple sauce.)

Star of David Hanukkah cards

Age range
Five to eleven.

Group size
Individuals.

What you need
Thin card offcuts, sheets of thin card or paper (A4 size approximately), crayons, scissors, adhesive, pens or pencils.

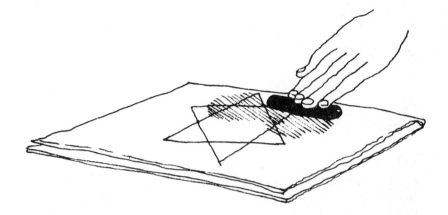

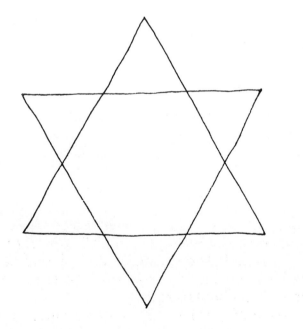

What to do
Cut two equilateral triangles of equal size (about 8 cm sides) from the card offcuts. Stick one over the other as shown to form a Star of David. Fold the sheet of paper in half to make a card and place the star inside. Using a crayon make a careful rubbing of the star on the front of the card. Open the card and write a greeting inside.

Menorah design

The menorah used at Hanukkah holds nine candles, the one in the centre being used to light the other eight candles, one for each night of Hanukkah.

Age range
Seven to eleven.

Group size
Individuals.

What you need
One sheet of A5 white paper per person and one A4 sheet of another colour per person, adhesive, scissors, pencils, copies of the half menorah on page 122.

What to do
Using the pattern on page 122, draw half a menorah along the longer edge of the white paper. Cut out the menorah carefully keeping the background paper intact. Keep both the menorah shape and the paper from which it was cut. Holding the coloured paper horizontally fold down the centre to form two equal sized rectangles. Unfold the coloured paper. Stick the white paper from which menorah was cut to one side of the coloured paper taking care to match the edges and placing the cut or open side of the white paper along the fold in the coloured paper. Stick the white paper menorah to the other side of the coloured paper, matching the white candlesticks to the holes from which they were cut. Leave the design to dry flat.

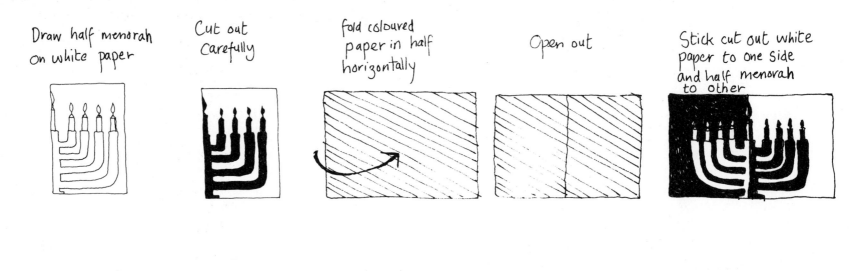

Draw half menorah on white paper

Cut out carefully

fold coloured paper in half horizontally

Open out

Stick cut out white paper to one side and half menorah to other

1   2   3   4   5

St Nicholas' Day

St Nicholas was an early saint whose legendary quality was that of generosity demonstrated through the giving of gifts to the poor. His feast day is 6 December and traditionally he arrives in Amsterdam with his servants and parades through the city. Eventually 'Sinter Klaas' became known as Santa Claus and his visits began to take place on Christmas Eve.

Clothes for 'Santa'

Age range
Seven upwards.

Group size
Individuals.

What you need
Fabrics of various kinds, pens, scissors, paper, adhesive, picture of Santa or Saint Nicholas.

What to do
Discuss with the children how Santa is usually shown wearing clothes suitable for cold climates. Ask them to design a costume for him suitable for hotter climates.

In addition the children could try to think what present they would most like to give Santa or Saint Nicholas.

St Lucia's Day

St Lucia's Day is celebrated in Sweden and several other European countries on 13 December and marks the beginning of the Christmas season. St Lucia was put to death by the Romans for her Christian beliefs fifteen hundred years ago and was later made a saint. Lucia means 'light' and she has become the queen of lights.

In Italy big bonfires are built and there are processions by torch and candlelight. In Sweden, a young girl, often the oldest daughter dresses up in a long white dress around which is tied a red sash. On her head she wears a crown of evergreens adorned with candles. She serves coffee and a special kind of twisted bun with raisins to her family first thing in the morning. These buns are twisted into different shapes; some are called 'Lucia Cats' – Lussekatter.

Star boy hats

Age range
Five to eleven.

Group size
Individuals.

What you need
Sugar paper approximately 30 cm × 45 cm for each person, gold/silver paper, stapler, adhesive, wool/ribbon, scissors, plate or similar to make circle.

What to do
Draw a large circle on paper and cut it out. Stick or staple into a cone shape. Cut some stars from gold or silver paper and then stick to the hat. Cut two ties from ribbon or wool and tape one to each side of the hat at the lower rim to tie under the chin.

(For Lucia crowns for girls see *Bright Ideas Christmas Activities*.)

Lucia cats

Age range
Five to eleven.

Group size
Small group.

What you need
Mixing bowls – one large and one small, wooden spoon, sieve, spatula, board, baking sheet, ruler, egg beater, teaspoon.

Ingredients
325 g flour,
¼ tsp baking powder,
2 small eggs,
125 g sugar,
250 g margarine,
1 tsp vanilla extract,
yellow food colour without harmful additives (from health food shop),
small packet raisins.

What to do
Make sure hands are clean. Preheat oven to 350 °F/ 180 °C/gas mark 4. Grease the baking tray. Sieve the flour and baking powder together. Beat the eggs gently in small bowl.

Cream together the sugar and margarine in a large bowl. Stir in the vanilla extract and beaten eggs and several drops of yellow food colouring. Now add the sieved flour a little at a time, mixing well. Blend the dough with your hands and shape it into a ball.

Remove from bowl and put on lightly floured board. Dust hands with flour. Now take a small ball of dough and roll it into a snake. Continue rolling until it is about 25 cm long and 1 cm wide. Curl one end of dough snake around on itself as shown. Bend the other end in the opposite direction. Put a raisin in the middle of each curl.

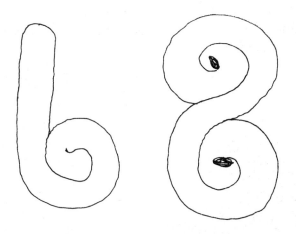

Transfer each biscuit on to the baking sheet with a spatula. Bake for seven to ten minutes until golden in colour. Remove and leave to cool. (Makes about 25 biscuits.)

Spring term

New Year – Hogmanay

The New Year offers opportunities for new beginnings and generally the customs related to it reflect this thinking. There is a tradition of making New Year's resolutions – or at least considering the possibility of changing or improving one's life for the coming year.

In Scotland the celebration of the New Year, Hogmanay, tends to exceed the celebrations for Christmas and is the most important festival. Each family gathers at the home of its oldest member and open house is held for friends and relations. There is much preparation for Hogmanay; homes are cleaned and Scottish treats such as scones, shortbread, New Year black buns and Hogmanay oat cakes are baked. The black buns are rich pastries filled with nuts, raisins and spices.

Some people believe that their luck for the coming year is determined by the first person who enters their home after midnight on Hogmanay Eve. If this 'first footer' is a dark-haired male stranger carrying a piece of coal, the household should have luck and good fortune in the coming year.

One of the traditional images of the New Year is that of Old Father Time carrying a scythe contrasted by a young cherub holding an hour glass containing the seeds of time for the coming year.

Janus was an ancient Roman god. He had two faces, one looking forward and one looking back and so he could see the future and the past at the same time. He was the god of doors and gates and so of beginnings and openings. The month of January was named after him and was sacred to him.

Janus mask

Age range
Five to eight.

Group size
Individuals.

What you need
Large brown paper bag for each child, pencils, scissors, coloured pens, paints, brushes, adhesive, assorted coloured paper.

What to do
   To make the mask put the bag over the children's heads to find out where to put the eyes, nose and mouth of the forward looking face. Mark the positions of these, remove the bag and draw in the features, using paint or pens to add more details. Allow them to dry. Make holes in the outlines of the eyes, nose and mouth with scissors. Cut out each shape. Paint a backward looking face on the other side of the bag.
   Cut strips of paper for the hair. Curl the strips around a pencil and stick to the bag.
   Add a wreath of green leaves by cutting individual leaves and joining them together by overlapping and sticking into a chain to wrap around the whole mask.

Baking shortbread

Age range
Five plus.

Group size
Small groups.

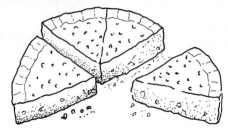

What you need
Mixing bowl, scales, wooden spoon, two baking trays, rolling pin, blunt knife, fork.

Ingredients
200 g butter (softened),
150 g caster sugar,
350 g plain flour.

What to do
Pre-heat the oven to 350 °F/180 °C/gas mark 4. Cream the butter with the wooden spoon and gradually beat in the sugar, about 25 g at a time.
   Add all the flour and knead with the hands to form a smooth dough. Grease the baking trays. Divide the dough mix into two and put each half in the centre of a tray. Roll out each half gently to form a circle. Now carefully divide each circle into eight pieces by scoring lightly with the knife. You can use the other end of the knife to make the fluted edges all round the circles. Prick the top approximately every 2 cm. Place the tray in the oven for about 20–25 minutes until the shortbread turns a golden colour. Leave to cool and then cut out the pieces.
   When ready to eat, you may like to ask the children to sit on the floor in a circle and crossing arms shake hands with the person on either side. Then serve the shortbread.

Old Year, New Year

Age range
Six plus.

Group size
Small groups.

What you need
Small pieces of card, writing materials, space for movement, percussion instruments.

What to do
Discuss with the children the idea that New Year is a time for reflecting on things past and making new starts. One child could act as the Old Year, and she should point out some of the things that have been done over the past year (that the school or class has done, or individual things). The other members of the group, New Year, can then suggest ways to make changes for the better and think of new plans.

They can then write a few realistic resolutions or personal aims on the pieces of card. These can be displayed against a model or picture of Old Father Time and the New Year Cherub, or alternatively suspended from the Janus masks which can be hung across the room (see page 44).

This activity could be extended by movement ideas; ie the Old Year would move very slowly, possibly stiffly and in a tired way. In contrast the New Year would move lightly and with energy and enthusiasm. The children could decide which percussion instruments would be appropriate to accompany each of these movements.

Tu b'Shevat

In Israel, this spring holiday falls in January or February (the fifteenth day of the Hebrew month Shevat). It is a special day for planting trees and it marks the end of winter. The children parade through the streets carrying gardening tools. They then go to plant trees, dance, sing and play games.

Trees are very important in Israel and according to custom when a boy is born Jewish fathers plant a cedar tree, and a cypress tree when a girl is born.

Folded trees

Age range
Seven to eleven.

Group size
Individuals.

What you need
Green paper (approximately A4 size), pencils, crayons, scissors.

What to do
Fold the paper backwards and forwards in accordian folds as shown.

Start at the folded edge and draw the outline of half a tree. Make sure that at least some of the branches touch the fold. Carefully cut through all the layers of paper and cut round the tree shape. Unfold the paper.

If they wish, the children can decorate the branches with birds, nests or blossoms.

Tree talk

Age range
Four to seven.

Group size
Whole class divided into small groups.

What you need
Pencils, paper.

What to do
Talk with the children about the trees growing around the school. Do they like seeing them? Why do they think they are important? Then ask each group to compile a list of reasons why they think trees should be conserved. One member of each group could be asked to act as scribe.

You could then ask the children to imagine that the council had decided to cut down all the trees near the school. They must then compose a letter to the local authority saying why the trees must be saved.

Word tree

Age range
Five to seven.

Group size
Small groups.

What you need
Paper, pencils, large outline of a tree for each group, paper leaves.

What to do
Ask the children to think of as many 'tree' words as they can, considering names of parts of a tree as well as words to describe trees. (They should first have the opportunity to observe a tree closely.)

Get each child to write down all the words they can. Then ask each group to pool their words and write each word on a small paper leaf. Stick the leaves to the tree to provide the foliage.

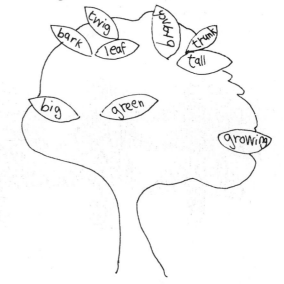

Tie-dye tree patterns

Age range
Six to eleven.

Group size
Individuals or small group.

What you need
Cold water dyes, washing soda, salt, plastic buckets, rubber gloves, white cotton material, marbles, string.

What to do
Give each child a square of cotton (about 60 cm square) for each design.

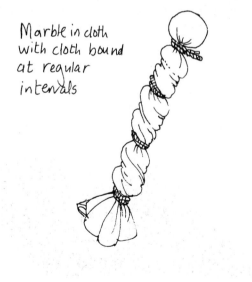

Marble in cloth with cloth bound at regular intervals

Place a marble in the centre of the square and wrap the cloth up (in similar fashion to folding an umbrella). Bind string tightly around the folded cloth just above the marble. Bind string at intervals along the cloth. Wearing rubber gloves, dye the cloth according to the instructions on the dye packet.

tie-dye pattern of concentric rings

Wash the cloth thoroughly. Iron and mount the pattern which should look like the pattern of concentric rings which represent the annual growth rings found in the cross section of a tree trunk.

Saraswati Puja

This Hindu festival is celebrated in January or February on the day of Basanta Panchami. (Basanta is the season which follows winter and Panchami means fifth day – here, after the new moon.) The day of Basanta Panchami is kept as a day of worship of the goddess Saraswati but the customs and celebrations vary from place to place in India.

The spring season, Basanta, officially begins on that day too and it is the time when the huge mustard fields are yellow with flowers; thus yellow is also called 'basant' and it is a special colour during this season.

The goddess Saraswati is the goddess of learning and the arts and so the festival has two aspects: a day of worship of the goddess of learning and as Basanta Panchami, a forerunner to the festival of Holi. In Britain the festival is usually performed within family homes.

In India the image of the goddess is placed on a raised platform and the area of floor in front is decorated with beautiful patterns called 'alpana'. This is usually done by the housewives and young women; they dip the ring finger of the right hand in a thick paste of powdered rice and water and draw the pattern straight on to the floor.

Alpana floor pattern

Age range
Five to eleven.

Group size
Individuals.

What you need
Dark coloured paper, mixture of rice-powder and water (white powder paint could be used instead).

What to do
Explain to the children that 'alpana' patterns are usually made by the women and that the patterns are drawn without guidelines. These are done after dipping the ring finger into the rice powder/water paste. Let them experiment using their ring finger to spread the mixture and when they can manage this they can draw out a design on their dark paper.

Chinese New Year

As the Chinese follow a lunar calendar, the Chinese New Year (Yuan Tan) falls on a different day (the first day of the lunar calendar) each year; but it usually occurs between mid January and mid February. It is the most important festival in the Chinese calendar and lasts for 15 days. Chinese communities all over the world celebrate the New Year with festivities at home and in the streets. Its origins are religious and there are rituals in honour of domestic gods but much of the festivity is secular.

Each New Year is named after an animal, one of the twelve who ran in the Jade Emperor's race and the first year in the sequence is the year of the rat.

Just before New Year people clean their homes thoroughly to wash and brush away any bad luck. Red decorations are hung on doors or windows usually bearing the New Year's message 'longevity, prosperity, happiness and harmony'. Most families also decorate their homes with a flowering branch such as peach blossom.

New Year is a time for visiting; everyone has new clothes and the front door is kept open. Children receive gifts of good luck money in small red envelopes often with gold lettering on called Hung Pao. Special foods are eaten: a traditional New Year's pastry filled with nuts, fruits such as oranges and tangerines (symbols of long life), and vegetable dishes.

Lucky money envelope

Age range
Six to eleven.

Group size
Individuals.

What you need
Red paper (approximately A4 size), gold paper, crayons or pens, scissors, adhesive, pencils, copies of envelope outline from page 123.

What to do
The younger children can use a cut-out copy of the envelope as a template to draw round on their red paper. Older children can use the template as a guide, doing their own measuring and ruling.

When the outline envelope is ready, fold and stick the sides together as shown. Fold over the bottom flap and stick together, then fold over the top flap but leave this open.

The Chinese greeting 'Kung Hai Fat Choy' (Happy New Year) can then be written in gold crayon or pen on the front of the envelope. Older children can try to draw the Chinese symbols or cut them out from gold paper and stick them on to the envelope.

Paper weaving

Age range
Six to eleven.

Group size
Individuals.

What you need
Red paper about A4 size or 30 cm square, thin strips (2 cm) of white, yellow or gold paper. (The colours can be reversed using these as the backing sheet and cutting red strips.)

What to do
The Chinese are very skilled weavers particularly using bamboo, flax, rattan and silk. Let the children try some paper weaving as part of their New Year activities.

Use the red paper sheet as a loom. Fold this in half top to bottom (if rectangular) and draw a line across about 3 cm from the open edge. Now from the centre fold draw lines to this line about 2 cm apart. Cut along the vertical lines and open the paper out.

Now weave the strips in and out of the 'loom' sticking the ends down when completed.

New Year cards

Age range
Five to eleven.

Group size
Individuals.

What you need
Red paper or thin card, gold crayons, pens or paper, scissors.

What to do
Each person needs a piece of red paper or thin cardboard. Most Chinese New Year cards have a red background on which are pictures including dragons or the lion dance in some form; peach blossom or kumquat; the symbols for good luck, happiness, long life, prosperity and good fortune and the traditional greeting 'Kung Hai Fat Choy' – 'Happy New Year'.

Let the children design their own cards using some of these suggestions, outlining and embellishing their designs with gold crayons, pens or paper.

You can make good luck scrolls that can be hung up in a similar way but the red paper will need to be cut longways: 30 cm × 10 cm is a suitable size. Write the symbols from top to bottom.

Chinese addition

Age range
Seven plus.

Group size
Individuals.

What you need
Copies of the Chinese addition sheet (see page 126), pencils.

What to do
Ask the children to work out the addition sums on the sheet. Once they have completed these they could try writing some more for others to try.

Paper dragons

Age range
Six to eleven.

Group size
Individuals.

What you need
Strips of paper approximately 1 m × 3 cm in different colours, small pieces of coloured paper, adhesive, small spills (plastic straws will do), pens.

What to do
Each child needs two strips of paper in contrasting colours — red and yellow for example. Lay the end of one strip at right angles over the end of the other and fix together with a dab of adhesive. Now fold each strip alternately over the other until all the paper has been folded. Fix these ends together with adhesive. Stick a spill to each end.

Now make a small dragon face and stick this to one end of the folded strip over the spill. Make a tail and stick it to other end. The dragon can be made to move using the spills to extend and manipulate the body.

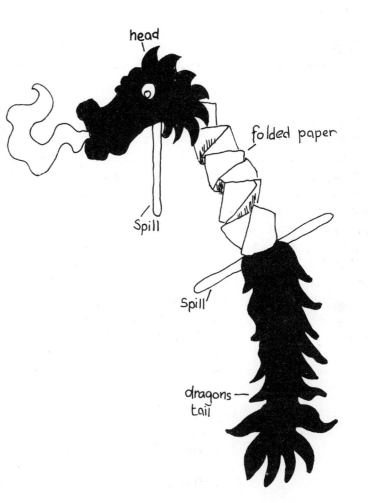

Animal wheel

Age range
Seven to eleven.

Group size
Twelve children.

What you need
Large sheet of paper or thin card, paints, pencils, pens, coloured papers, collage materials, adhesive, scissors, compasses, long ruler, copies of the Chinese animal years on pages 124 and 125.

What to do
Tell the children the names of the twelve animals after which the Chinese years are named. Decide who is going to make which picture. Draw a large circle on the paper and divide this into twelve equal parts. (You may wish to do this for the younger children but a pair of older children could do this themselves.)

Each member of the group then makes a picture of the animal chosen to fit the wheel and writes the appropriate name in large letters on a strip of paper.

Cut out the animals and stick them around the wheel in the following order starting at the top and working clockwise: the rat, the ox, the tiger, the hare (or rabbit), the dragon, the snake, the horse, the ram (or sheep), the monkey, the rooster, the dog and the pig. Stick the names above the animals round the circumference of the wheel.

Now can the children work out which years belong to which animals? They could start from 1912 – a year of the rat. There is more than one way they could do this – see which ways your children can discover.

When they have worked out the cycle up to the current year, they will need to enter these in a list under the appropriate animal. By looking at the year in which they were born, the children can find out which animal rules it. They could also do this for friends, parents etc. Are they like the creatures in any way? (See page 124 and 125 for characteristics of each animal.)

Teng Chieh

Teng Chieh or the lantern festival takes place two weeks after the start of the Chinese New Year – the fifteenth day of the first full moon – and marks the end of the New Year celebrations. It celebrates the return of the light and the coming of spring.

Lanterns representing dragons, lions, fish and tigers are hung in the streets and in shops and children go in procession carrying lighted lanterns.

The high spot of the festivities is the dance of the lion or dragon. For this the costume is made from a framework of bamboo and covered with brightly coloured and embroidered silk (or paper) and is often a hundred feet long.

Chinese lanterns

Age range
Five to eleven.

Group size
Individuals.

What you need
White or coloured paper (at least A4 size), paint, pens or crayons, adhesive or staples, string, sticks, paper strips, ruler.

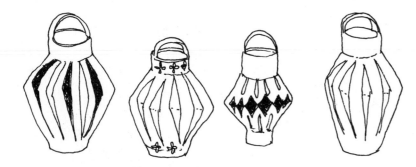

What to do
Fold the sheet of paper in half lengthwise; open and decorate. Draw a straight line on one side of the folded paper about 2 cm from the open edge.

Cut slits along folded edge to pencil line. Unfold the sheet and roll around lengthwise so that the two short sides meet. Stick or staple these sides together.

Add a strip of paper to one end of the cylinder to form a handle; this can be glued or stapled.

Tie one end of a piece of string to a stick and the other end around the lantern handle. Alternatively if you wish, the lanterns can be strung across the room rather than being attached to sticks.

Fish lanterns

Age range
Six to eleven.

Group size
Individuals.

What you need
Coloured tissue or lightweight paper, adhesive, pipe-cleaners, coloured foil and paper scraps, scissors, sticks, string.

What to do
Get the children to cut out two matching fish shapes from the tissue-paper and stick along the sides and tail to form a hollow fish. Stuff small scraps of paper in the body to keep the shape.

Shape the pipe-cleaner into a ring and glue around the mouth edge. Leave to dry. Decorate the fish with foil and coloured scraps. When dry attach the fish to the stick with string.

Lion's head and body

Age range
Five to eleven.

Group size
Small groups.

What you need
Cardboard, crêpe paper, lightweight fabric, adhesive, chicken wire, acrylic paints, pictures of lion dance procession if possible, paste, newspaper, coloured tissue-paper, paper plates, needle and thread (optional).

What to do
Show the children the pictures to give them ideas. First make the head, using the chicken wire to form the basic shape. Cover the structure with newspaper soaked in paste. For the last layer use small pieces of tissue-paper. When the adhesive has dried, paint the head and add features.

To make the body, use a long piece of fabric or crêpe paper. Stitch or stick the edges together. Make hoops from thin card (or insert paper plates) to give the body shape. Add the tail and legs from card and crêpe paper. Join head and body together. The whole creature can

then be suspended from the ceiling. Alternatively, you may wish to make a lion large enough for the children to dress up in and have a procession. If so, leave the bottom of the body open and leave out the hoops.

Candlemas

Candlemas day falls on 2 February and takes its name from the blessing of candles on that day for use in church during the forthcoming year. It celebrates the feast of the presentation of Christ in the Temple when Simeon spoke of him as 'A light to lighten the Gentiles'. Christians used to light candles for Mary and the baby Jesus which were blessed, and in some places blessed candles are still given to the congregation on this day.

An old belief has it that all hibernating animals wake up on Candlemas day and come out to see if it is still winter. If it is a sunny day the animal will see its shadow and be frightened so it returns for a further 40 days of sleep. If it is cloudy the animal will not see its shadow or become frightened so it stays above the ground. People then say we will have an early spring. In America this day is celebrated as Groundhog Day.

Put the candles out

Age range
Seven plus.

Group size
Small groups.

What you need
Small candles, non combustible containers eg jars, matches, saucers, timer. Adult supervision.

What to do
Place the candles on saucers and light them. When they are burning well, cover each one with a jar. The children should then observe what happens. Ask them to make predictions as to what will happen; will all the candles burn for the same length of time?

Time how long it takes for each candle to go out. If all the candles are the same size, can the children explain why one may burn for longer? Does the size and shape of the container covering the candle make a difference?

Shadow guessing game

Age range
Five plus.

Group size
Small groups.

What you need
Projector or flashlight, screen – a large sheet of white paper will do, a variety of objects in a box.

What to do
Each child takes their turn to place an object from the box near the projector or light source. The other members of the group have to then guess what the object is that is casting the shadow on the screen.

Individuals could also select one of the objects and experiment making a shadow shorter or longer, bigger or smaller.

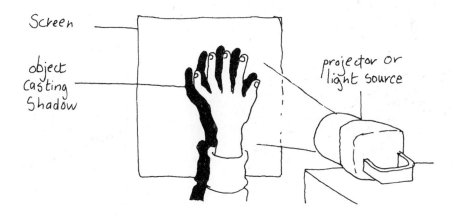

Screen

object Casting Shadow

projector or light source

Mardi Gras

Mardi Gras is also known around the world as Carnival or Shrove Tuesday and this colourful festival falls in February. In many Christian countries the last few days before Lent are a time of merry-making and great feasting. People dress up in fancy costumes or wear masks and there is often dancing and singing in the streets. Originally Carnival was an old Italian festival lasting from Twelfth Night to Ash Wednesday. Today the celebration of Carnival takes a variety of forms in different parts of the world, often being planned long in advance.

In France the great Mardi Gras (Fat Tuesday) procession is held with floats and a flower battle; and in the south of the country there is a carnival king with a court of clowns.

In Germany the carnival is called Faschling; masked processions take place and doughnuts and pretzels are eaten.

One of the most famous carnivals takes place in Trinidad in the West Indies. This started in the nineteenth century and is now one of the year's most important events. The celebrations begin on the Monday with a fancy dress procession through the streets to the sounds of steel bands playing calypso music. In the evening the costumes are judged, fireworks are set off and people dance all night. On the next day, Shrove Tuesday, there is an even more dramatic parade led by those wearing the winning costumes.

Musical instruments

Age range
Five to eleven.

Group size
Individuals/pairs.

What you need A
Plastic buckets or bowls (large coffee tins would do), elastic bands, strong plastic bags or plastic sheeting or acetate film.

What to do
If you are using acetate film, soak it in water first for a few seconds. Carefully stretch the plastic sheeting or soaked acetate film over the top of the tin or bowl making sure that it overlaps the sides all round. Fix an elastic band around the rim. To get a good sound the plastic or acetate film must be stretched smoothly without any wrinkles. The instrument is played by tapping lightly with the fingers.

Maracas are traditionally South American but they make a splendid sound for a carnival band.

What you need B
Dried rice or peas, buttons, nails etc, sticky tape, washing-up liquid bottles, dowelling, paint, varnish or PVA adhesive.

What to do
Let the children experiment with various different 'fillings' for their maracas to see what different sounds can be produced. When they have decided on their sound put some of the noise-maker into the washing-up bottle and ram a piece of dowel into the neck to make a handle. This should then be secured around the join with sticky tape. Paint the outside brightly with thick paint and when dry a coating of undiluted PVA will give a varnished finish.

Carnival band

Age range
Five to eleven.

Group size
Whole class.

What you need
Home-made instruments, steel band music.

What to do
Let the children listen to the traditional steel band music paying particular attention to the rhythm. Then let them experiment with their instruments trying to keep with the beat. Once they are able to do this they may like to try to work out sequences with the drums playing at one time, then the maracas and both instruments together.

Valentine's Day

This festival is held annually on 14 February. Before St Valentine became the saint of lovers, a festival was held in ancient Rome to honour the god, Pan. The Romans called their festival Lupercalia and one of the customs was that the names of the young men and women were put in a box and shaken up. They were then drawn out like a lottery to choose token sweethearts.

It is also said that in the third century AD, an important member of the church, some say the Bishop Valentine of Rome, was put to death on the eve of Lupercalia for his beliefs. One story says that after his arrest he fell in love with the gaoler's daughter and when he was led out for execution, he left a note for her signed merely 'Your Valentine'.

Traditionally this date has become a day on which lovers make their feelings known and country lore has it that it is the day on which birds choose their mates. Birds, hearts, flowers and lace are the images of the festival and sentimental poems are often used for inscriptions on cards.

Pop-up Valentines cards

Age range
Seven plus.

Group size
Individuals.

What you need
Thin A4 size card for each person, scissors, pens, pencils, thin fabric scraps or coloured papers etc for decorations.

What to do
Get the children to cut out their card shape as shown. Suggest that they lightly fold their sheet in half to start, then open it flat and draw the heart shape. They should then cut out the whole shape and fold as shown.

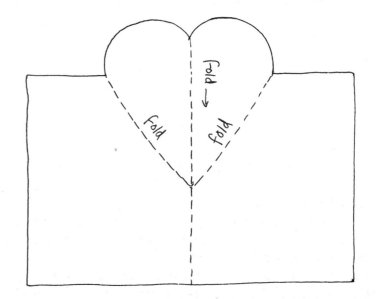

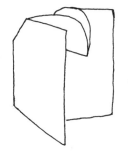

design on paper or thin card. Get them to leave tabs around the edge of each item of clothing. The clothes can be fixed on to the teddy outline by bending the tabs around the body. A hat could be added by making a slit and slipping it over the bear's head.

After the Valentine is folded they can add their own greeting and decorate their card.

Teachers may prefer to make a larger master sheet on A4 paper and provide children with a ready-made outline.

Design a Valentine costume

Age range
Five plus.

Group size
Individuals.

What you need
Thin card, paper, pens, scissors.

What to do
Explain that cuddly toys are often given as a symbol of love on Valentine's Day. The children can then design a Valentine costume for a teddy.

First get them to draw a teddy outline on the thin card and cut this out. Then each child should draw his clothes

fold down

Alternatively the children could draw directly on to their cut-out bears, adding whatever costume they wish.

Scrambled Valentine words

Age range
Seven plus.

Group size
Individuals or pairs.

What you need
Pink card, pencils.

What to do
Cut out heart shapes on thin card – pink if possible; write scrambled Valentine words – one on each heart. Make several sets of each so that a number of pairs can work at the same time. Put each set in an envelope.

  The children then have to work out what each word is and write it on their paper. (You might wish to provide them with a page of outline heart shapes – one to write each word in).

  Suitable words could be: waror – arrow; vole – love; thaer – heart; pudci – cupid; tennilave – valentine; grinadl – darling; stopoxb – postbox; birbno – ribbon.

Other quick language ideas
● Draw and cut out a number of heart shapes. Outline each with red pen and also draw an interlocking cut across each one in the same place in a horizontal direction. Write compound words – half on each part of the heart. Cut them in half. The children then have to mend the broken hearts.

  Some suggestions for words: milkman, farmyard, grandmother, fireworks, toothbrush, teapot, playground, football, newspaper, birthday.
● How many words can you think of which contain the word 'heart'?
● Using the letters in the word 'Valentine' how many words can you make?

Measuring heartbeats

Age range
Nine plus.

Group size
Small groups.

What you need
Timer for seconds, recording sheets, pencils.

What to do
First the children will need to find the position of the heart in the body and feel the beat. How many times does it beat in 15 seconds? How many times does it beat in one minute? Explain that heartbeat can also be felt as a pulse and then let pairs take each other's pulse for 15 seconds/ one minute. (This activity will need to be supervised carefully.) The results should be recorded for each person.

Now ask them to do some exercise – say 30 star jumps – and record the pulse-rate straight after the exercise. What changes do they note? Whose pulse has changed most? and least?

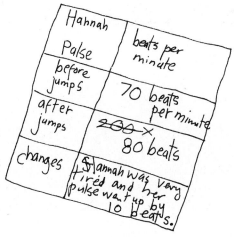

Hannah	beats per minute
Pulse before jumps	70 beats per minute
after jumps	2̶0̶0̶ X 80 beats
changes	Hannah was very tired and her pulse want up by 10 beats.

Purim

Purim is a Jewish festival usually falling in late February or early March. It is one of the happiest of the Jewish festivals and is the last in the Jewish calendar before Passover, four weeks later. It is a reminder of how the Jewish people living in Persia were saved from death by Esther.

Purim is named from the word 'Pur' which means dice or 'lots'. The story is told in the book of Esther of how a wicked man, Haman, wanted to kill all the Jews living in the Persian Empire because he thought one of them, Mordecai, had been disrespectful in refusing to bow before him because he had an image of an idol on his cloak. So Haman threw dice (cast lots) to decide on which day the Jews should die. On the allotted day however, Esther overcame Haman's plan by her own guile at a specially arranged banquet.

The book of Esther was written on a scroll called the Megillah.

Make a Megillah

Age range
Five to eleven.

Group size
Pairs.

What you need
Longish cardboard rolls, long strips of paper, adhesive, pens or crayons, pencils, coloured beads or similar, gold paper or spray.

What to do
Tell the children the background story, explaining what a Megillah is.

Ask them to work in pairs and on the long strips of paper, draw pictures to represent the story, with captions. They should start from the right as the Jews read the scroll from the right to left. Then cover the cylinders and beads with gold paper (or spray) and stick beads to the top and bottom of the cylinders.

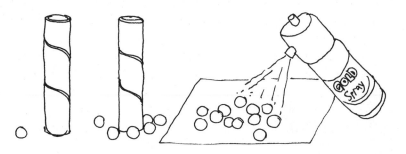

When dry stick the left-hand end of the paper to one cylinder. Roll up the paper and stick the right-hand end to the other cylinder. Unroll to reveal the story.

St David's Day

St David is the patron saint of Wales and St David's Day is celebrated on 1 March, although the reason for choosing this day as 'his day' is not clear. However, it is very much a Welsh cultural festival and a time for music and song.

David lived during the sixth century in South-West Wales and was an important churchman, living a simple life and representing the Christian faith. He established a monastery at a place now known as St David's – a small cathedral city.

There are many stories related to his qualities as a preacher and miracle worker. David eventually became archbishop of Wales.

It is customary for Welsh people to wear a leek on St David's day, although a daffodil is often worn instead.

Make music 1

Age range
Three plus.

Group size
Individuals or whole class.

What you need
A supply of cheap combs, stiff tissue-paper.

What to do
Each person should fold a small sheet of tissue-paper around a comb and then hum through the tissue, lips slightly apart. When the children have had time to experiment they can try to play simple tunes.

Make music 2

Age range
Six plus.

Group size
Small groups.

What you need
String or nylon line, two posts, cups and mugs, beaters.

What to do
Tie a line between two vertical posts and suspend the cups in a row from the line. The children can take turns in gently striking each cup with the beater (a stick will do). What different sounds do the cups make? Why do they think this is?

Encourage the children to subtract and add cups to obtain the widest range of notes possible. Can anyone work out a simple tune?

Make music 3

Age range
Six plus.

Group size
Small groups.

What you need
String or nylon line, two posts, nails of varying lengths and thicknesses, twist wires (as sold for freezer bag sealing).

What to do
Suspend the nails from the line using the twist wires. Ask the children to experiment with the sounds produced. Can they hang them in order from that producing the lowest sound to that making the highest sound? Do some nails 'ring' for longer than others? Why might this be?

St David's Day dragon

Age range
Six plus.

Group size
Whole class.

What you need
Large frieze paper, adhesive, magazines, a variety of red papers, pens, pencils, paints, scissors, trays or flat boxes for collecting paper.

What to do
First ask a pair of children to draw out on the frieze paper a large outline of a dragon. The other members of the class can search through the magazines for pages with red areas and cut or tear them out. These should be collected in the flat boxes. They can then paste the red paper on to the dragon, overlapping the pieces to give a scaly effect. When the whole body and head have been filled in, the features can be painted or drawn on with pens; don't forget the claws!

Hina Matsuri

This is the Japanese doll festival or Peach festival, and is celebrated on 3 March. It is also a time when peach blossoms are usually in full bloom. Just before the day itself, treasured heirloom dolls, exquisitely dressed in embroidered silk costumes are arranged carefully on a tierlike platform in a special place in the home of a Japanese family with a daughter.

The emperor and empress dolls are placed on the top shelf and ladies-in-waiting and their attendants are arranged on lower shelves. On the bottom shelf are placed little musical instruments and lacquered miniature furniture. Peach blossoms are arranged all round them.

The custom originated over 300 years ago in the Japanese Imperial Court. Nowadays the family celebrates with a special meal, often soup, fish, hishimochi (a diamond-shaped rice cake), and shirozake (rice wine). Girls invite their friends over to see their collections. It is the custom for Japanese parents to present their daughter with the first china doll at birth and the collection goes with her when she marries. The dolls are greatly treasured and become very valuable.

Long ago in Japan parents made paper dolls and wrote their children's names on them. It was thought that if they rubbed their children's bodies with the dolls, the paper would soak up all the illness that might come during the next year. The dolls were taken to the nearest river and floated away in the hope that they would carry all the diseases with them.

Hina origami dolls

Age range
Seven plus.

Group size
Individuals.

What you need
Coloured paper cut into 15 cm squares, scissors, thin white card, adhesive, felt-tipped pens. Optional: cardboard boxes, red felt or paper, tissue-paper, mastic adhesive.

What to do
If you wish to make the whole set of 15 dolls, the set comprises: one emperor, one empress, three ladies-in-waiting, five musicians, two imperial guards, and three courtiers. Allocate each child one doll.

Give each person two squares of different coloured paper: the emperor will have one colour combination, the empress another, the ladies-in-waiting a third, and the musicians a fourth, and so on.

The children must then place their two squares of paper together on the diagonal, leaving about 1 cm border and fold in half along that diagonal, then unfold again.

Next fold up the bottom points so that they lie on the diagonal. Fold in the left-hand layers on a slant, then fold in the right-hand ones to lay on top of the left-hand ones.

The bottom edge is then folded backwards to allow the doll to stand.

Now draw the appropriate face on to the thin card, add the features with felt-tipped pens and cut out leaving a neck so that this can be pushed into the body part.

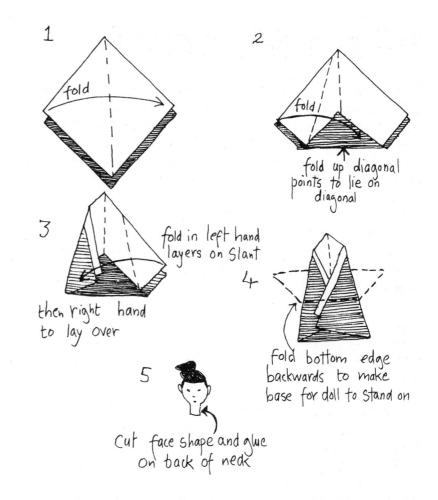

1 fold

2 fold / fold up diagonal points to lie on diagonal

3 fold in left hand layers on slant / then right hand to lay over

4 fold bottom edge backwards to make base for doll to stand on

5 Cut face shape and glue on back of neck

Glue the back of the neck and stick into the body at the top.

If you want to create the whole display, cover some boxes with red felt or paper and arrange in tiers – one for the emperor and empress, one for the ladies-in-waiting, one for the musicians and one for the guards and courtiers. Cut out some tissue-paper blossoms to decorate the tiers and fix the dolls to the stand with the mastic adhesive.

Doll day celebration

Age range
Five plus.

Group size
Variable.

What you need
The children and their favourite dolls.

What to do
Tell the children the background to the Hina festival and ask them to bring in their favourite doll. A display of these can be made in the hall and a selection of children can show their favourite doll to the others, telling its name and what makes it special. Those not actually talking should make labels bearing their own name and that of the doll to put on the display.

You could also have a large bowl of cold cooked rice for the children to sample; or better still one for each class which could be collected and taken on the way out of assembly to taste in the classroom.

The Japanese are very aware of good manners and behaviour to one another; their word for goodbye come back again is 'Sayonara'. A small group of children could demonstrate the Japanese leave-taking, saying the word and bowing politely from the waist, at the close of assembly. This should set the tone for polite manners to one another for the rest of the day.

Some Japanese words to learn:

please – dozo (DOH-zoh)
excuse me – shitsurei (SH'TSOO-reh-ee)
help – tasukete (tah-SKET-eh)
rice (cooked) – gohan (GOH-hahn)
tea – o-cha (oh-CHCH)
fish – sakana (sah-kah-NAH)
soup – o-suimono (oh-soo-ee-moh-NOH)

Holi

Holi is a Hindu spring festival which usually falls in March and the celebrations often last over three days. It is named after the demon goddess, Holika, who tried to kill Prahlad, a devotee of Vishnu who refused to believe that his own wicked father was God. The ripening of the first barley and wheat crops is also celebrated so it is a harvest festival too.

During the festival processions and dancing take place in the streets, coconuts are roasted and bonfires are lit. The idea of burning last year's rubbish and beginning afresh is another aspect of Holi which is also a fire festival. Another of the traditional customs is the throwing of coloured water or paint at passers by. People are allowed to be rude to those they normally respect: pupils may throw things at their teachers, for instance!

Fire pictures

Age range
Three to seven.

Group size
Individuals.

What you need
Icing sugar, water, paint brushes, activity paper, red and yellow paint, collage materials.

What to do
Mix the water and icing sugar to a thin, paint-like consistency. Cover a sheet of sugar paper with the solution, using a paint brush.

Sprinkle dots of fairly thin red and yellow paint on to the sheet. The wet surface should make the blobs of paint spread and run into each other giving a fiery effect.

People can also be added to the picture using the collage materials.

Paint sprinkle pictures

Age range
Five to eleven.

Group size
Individuals or small groups.

What you need
Large sheets of paper, PVA adhesive (in nozzled dispenser), brushes, powder paint.

What to do
Ask the children to make pictures of people and stick these to the large sheets of paper. When the pictures are completely dry, they can then dribble the adhesive over the paper and sprinkle dry powder paint over it.

Fire picture in words and music

Age range
Five to nine.

Group size
Whole class.

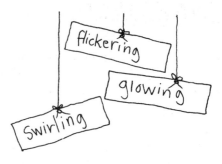

What you need
Red, yellow, orange, brown and grey paper, pens, thread, percussion instruments such as tambourines, triangles, cymbals, wood blocks.

What to do
First encourage the children to talk about fire and fiery words; try to get them to think of words which evoke each part of the bonfire; embers glowing or smouldering; flames jumping, flickering, leaping, blazing; sparks crackling, flying; smoke choking, swirling. First get the children to write the words on cut-outs of the appropriate parts of the bonfire. These can later be made into a bonfire mobile and suspended so that it moves in the air.

Select phrases for each part of the fire and decide on an order for speaking them, starting from the bottom of the fire. Divide the class into groups and each group in turn repeats their phrase in a rhythmic way to create a word sound picture. Then decide which instrument is most appropriate for each bonfire part, and after experimenting the children can create a sound picture using words and instruments, or if desired instruments only but thinking the words to keep the rhythm going.

Mothering Sunday

Mothering Sunday is celebrated on the fourth Sunday in Lent and seems to have no connection with the American May celebration of Mothering Sunday of only some 70 years standing.

In Britain the festival dates back to at least the seventeenth century when many happy reunions were achieved in the middle of a strictly observed fast. People became reunited with their churches and their families, and those 'in service' were given time off to visit their families or go 'a-mothering'. A posy of primroses or a simnel cake were regarded as acceptable gifts for a mother.

Nowadays 'Mother's Day' reflects a possibly commercial confusion with the American celebration. However it is a time when we can remind children to consider the role of the mother in their families. Traditionally, if wrongly, the mother's role is seen as cook, cleaner etc in addition to working outside the family. Children perhaps need to be encouraged to recognise the extent to which this has negated a mother's ability to develop both socially and intellectually as fully as she may have wished.

'Thank you, mum'

Age range
Six to eleven.

Group size
Individuals or whole class.

What you need
Pencils, rough paper, paper for final copy, pens or coloured pencils.

What to do
Ask the children to compose a poem for their mothers thanking her for the various things she does. Before trying to write their poems, the children should make a list of all the ways their mum helps and then make a rough draft poem. When they are happy with their poems, these can be written out neatly and decorated with pens or coloured pencils.

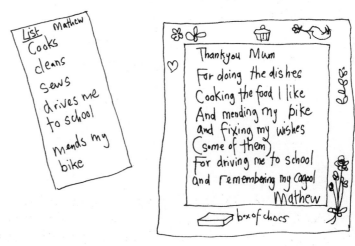

Mother's Day Card

Age range
Four to eleven.

Group size
Individuals or whole class.

What you need
Plain card, coloured pens, adhesive, the poem from previous activity, photograph of each child — one they already have (if this is impossible they could draw a self portrait.

What to do
Fold the plain card to make a traditional card form. Stick the photograph on to the front of the card and decorate around the picture to make a frame. Flower shapes is one obvious motif that could be used.

Stick the poem (from previous activity) inside the card and add any other greeting desired.

Huge help day

Age range
Five to eleven.

Group size
Whole class.

What you need
Pencils, paper (optional).

What to do
Ask the children to try to think how many things they can do to help their mums on Mothering Sunday. How many things does she do that the children could do for their mothers instead? What can they do to make their mums feel special on that day? You may like to suggest that they write down their ideas as a reminder.

St Patrick's Day

St Patrick is the patron saint of Ireland and he is remembered every year on 17 March. The festival is celebrated all over the world and has become a celebration of Irish culture. St Patrick used the shamrock, a three-leaved plant, to explain the Christian idea of God as three beings and one at the same time. Many people wear a bunch of shamrocks on St Patrick's Day.

There were many stories about St Patrick. One of the most famous tells how he managed to rid Ireland of all the snakes. It was said that once upon a time there were many snakes in Ireland and the people were very frightened of them. So St Patrick used his power to make the snakes follow him up to the top of a high cliff. He then drove them down over the other side into the sea. Since then no snakes have been seen in Ireland.

Snake movement

Age range
Five to eight.

Group size
Whole class.

What you need
An empty hall or lots of outdoor space.

What to do
Tell the children the story of St Patrick and the snakes. Ask them to think of words to describe the way snakes move. Suggest that they move their arms only first, to create snaky movements. Then using their whole bodies ask them to explore the space around them using snaky movements – twisting, turning, writhing etc. Once they have tried this they can move around the whole hall in a mass of snakes.

How might a snake move backwards, sideways, upwards, avoid another snake and so on? As a finale you may like to get them to follow you as St Patrick and get them to move in a definite pattern.

77

Colour mixing – making green

Age range
Seven plus.

Group size
Individuals.

What you need
Sugar paper, blue and yellow paints, black and white paints, brushes, mixing palettes, water, coloured magazines, pot plants or green leaves.

What to do
Ask the children to see how many different greens they can make by using different blue and yellow paints (modified by the white). The proportions of blue or yellow will also make differences.

Then ask them to see how the greens can be modified by using white or black paint. They can also try mixing black and white to produce grey and then mixing this with green in varying amounts to see the variety of colours created.

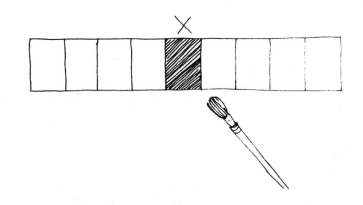

Follow-up 1
Using the colour magazines, ask the children to cut out squares of green colour of approximately 3 × 3 cm. They must then try to mix an exact copy of the cut-out square. Ask them to try this with several different colour green squares.

Follow-up 2
Look at the green colours in the plants and leaves, and discuss this with the children. They must then try to mix green colours to match the leaves of the plants they have.

Follow-up 3
Ask the children to draw a strip of nine squares on their paper. They must then mix a large quantity of their favourite shade of green. Paint the middle square of the strip with this colour, and mark it 'X'. From the square marked they should then mix their green with progressively more white, filling in the squares upwards until the colour turns white. Then mix black with the green in stages working downwards with the final bottom square becoming black.

Potato survey

Age range
Five plus.

Group size
Small group.

What you need
Pencils, paper, clip-board, graph paper, pens or crayons, rulers.

What to do
Potatoes used to form a very important part of the diet of the Irish people so take the opportunity to do a potato survey on St Patrick's day.

Ask the children to find out which way members of the group most like their potatoes cooked. Suggest they use the categories: boiled, roast, chips, mashed, baked in their jackets. When they have collected the information they must decide on the best way to represent this to the rest of the class. They could make a bar graph, a histogram, a pie chart, or draw sets or one set with sub-sets. You could leave the choice to the children, or ask them to see how many different ways they could present their findings.

St Patrick's Day story

Age range
Five plus.

Group size
Individuals.

What you need
Pencils, rough paper, copies of a shamrock outline for finished stories.

What to do
Let the children select a story title from these ideas (or they may have suitable one of their own) and work on a draft. When they are satisfied with what they have written, the story can be copied on to a shamrock sheet for display.
Possible titles:
    The strange man in green
    The magic potato
    The lucky leprechaun
    The shamrock surprise

Shamrock three times table

Age range
Six to eight.

Group size
Individuals.

What you need
Potato halves cut out to the shape of shamrocks,
green paint,
paper,
pencils,
adhesive,
scissors.

What to do
The children should first experiment with the potato and
paint so that they get a suitable consistency for printing.
When they have done this, ask them to print, starting from
the top of their paper, lines of shamrocks containing one
print, two prints and so on up to twelve prints. Leave the
prints to dry.

When dry the shamrock prints can be used to build up
the three times table:
1 shamrock – 3 leaves;
2 shamrocks – 6 leaves and so on.

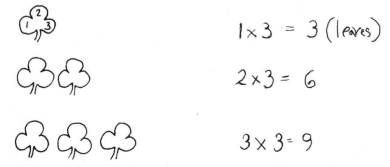

$$1 \times 3 = 3 \ (leaves)$$

$$2 \times 3 = 6$$

$$3 \times 3 = 9$$

$$4 \times 3 = 12$$

$$5 \times 3 = 15$$

$$6 \times 3 = 18$$

$$7 \times 3 = 21$$

$$8 \times 3 = 24$$

$$9 \times 3 = 27$$

$$10 \times 3 = 30$$

$$11 \times 3 = 33$$

$$12 \times 3 = 36$$

Passover

Passover is a Jewish spring festival and occurs in the Jewish month of Nisan. The Jewish name for the festival is Pesach, and it is one of the oldest festivals.

It falls in late March or early April and is essentially a family festival with the main celebration taking place in the home when the whole family gather in the first evening of the holiday for the Seder, a special meal held around the table. At this time the father of the family tells the children about that significant event when God intervened through Moses, to lead the Jewish people from slavery under Pharaoh's rule to freedom in the promised land.

Passover means 'passing over' and Jewish people also recall how the plague passed over their houses but entered those of the Egyptians bringing death to them and their animals. They remember too the miracle of their departure and the journey through the Red Sea which allowed them to pass through its waters but swallowed up the Egyptian army. They celebrate the bitterness of the many years of slavery and the sweetness of the freedom that followed.

Sweet, bitter and sour tasting

Age range
Five to eleven.

Group size
Small groups.

What you need
Different food items some sweet tasting, some bitter, some sour but including horseraddish, apple, parsley and cinnamon in numbered containers; paper, pens.

What to do
Each person in the group tastes each item in turn and decides whether it tastes bitter, sweet or sour. One person can act as recorder for the group. At the end the children can look to see if they all agreed on the categories.

As a follow-up the children can try to locate the sensitive parts of the tongue. They can do this by placing small amounts of each item on different parts of the tongue to see where it is actually tasted. They could then draw up a map of the tongue marking on the sensitive areas.

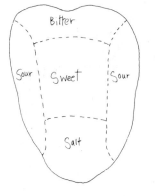

Collage of the ten plagues

Age range
Six plus.

Group size
Whole class.

What you need
Paints, coloured papers, scissors, pens, adhesive, crayons.

What to do
Tell the children the names of the plagues: blood, frogs, vermin (gnats), beasts (flies), cattle disease, boils, hail, locusts, darkness, death of the first born. Then decide how each could be represented pictorially (the children should do this with your guidance). Decide who will be responsible for making pictures of each of the plagues. The children can select the materials they think most suitable to make their pictures. When all the pictures are completed they can be cut out and displayed as a large frieze (possibly in the hall if you plan to have a Passover assembly).

Easter

The festival of Easter derives its name from the pre-Christian goddess symbols of spring: rebirth and fertility; the Saxon Eastre and the Old German Eostre. The ancient symbols – the egg and the hare – both representative of the return of new life after the sleep of winter, now carry the Christian association of Christ's Resurrection. Easter falls during March or April.

Egg rolling

Age range
Five to eleven.

Group size
Whole class.

What you need
A long stick for each person, hard-boiled eggs – one per participant, a large open space, chocolate Easter egg for the winner.

What to do
The participants must roll their eggs down the stretch of playground or field using the stick provided. (Alternatively you could use egg-sized pebbles for the race.) The winner could be presented with a chocolate Easter egg.

Egg hunt

Age range
Five to eleven.

Group size
Whole class.

What you need
Small chocolate eggs wrapped in foil (enough for two or three for each member of the group), basket for collecting.

What to do
Decide on the site of the egg hunt – classroom, an area of the playground (warn others!) or field. Acting as the 'hare' you should hide all the eggs but don't make them too easy to find. Once they are all hidden the children can start to search for them. Give them a certain time limit. You may like to ask them to bring all the found eggs to a central basket or container so that the eggs can be shared fairly at the end of the hunt.

At the end of the exercise the children could be asked to draw a plan of the hunt area, marking on the places where they found eggs.

Russian Paskha Easter cake

Age range
Six plus.

Group size
Small group.

What you need
Colander, saucer, wooden and metal spoon, sieve, three mixing bowls, one small saucepan, egg whisk, serving dish, cheesecloth, large clay flower pot, greaseproof paper, shallow dish, weight, refrigerator.

Ingredients
1 kg 350 g cottage cheese,
½ tsp vanilla essence,
60 g chopped candied fruit,
225 g unsalted butter (softened),
220 ml double cream,
220 g caster sugar,
4 egg yolks,
ice-cubes,
water,
55 g blanched chopped almonds,
50 g candied fruit,
50 g whole blanched almonds.

What to do
Close adult supervision and help will be needed. Drain the cottage cheese into a colander, cover with the greaseproof paper, put a saucer over the top and leave for two hours (you may want to do this in advance). Put the vanilla essence and chopped candied fruits into the smaller mixing bowl, stir thoroughly and leave the mixture for one hour. Rub the cheese through a fine sieve and put in a large bowl. Beat the softened butter into the cheese and put it aside.

Heat the cream in a saucepan over a high heat (with care), until small bubbles form round the edge of the pan. Put to one side.

Beat the sugar and egg yolks together in a mixing bowl until the mixture just runs off the whisk when lifted from the bowl. Add the hot cream slowly, beating at the same time.

Return the mixture to the pan and cook over a low heat stirring all the time until the mixture thickens to a custard-like consistency. Do not let the mixture boil. Remove from the heat.

Stir in the prepared candied fruits and place the pan in a large bowl filled with ice-cubes, covered with 5 cm of water.

Stir the mixture constantly with a metal spoon until thoroughly cooled. Gently mix into the cheese mixture and stir in chopped almonds.

Use the flower pot (it should have a hole in the base) as your mould. (The Russians have a special Paskha mould.) Place the pot in a shallow dish and line with damp cheesecloth – this needs to hang over the rim of the pot about 5 cm all round.

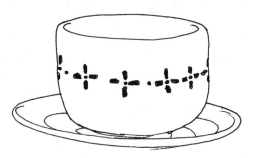

Pour in the batter mixture and fold the ends of the cheesecloth lightly over the top. Put a weight on top of the cheesecloth and place in the fridge for several hours.

To turn the cake out, unwrap the cloth from the top, place the flat serving dish upside down over the top of the pot and turn both over. The Paskha should slide out fairly easily. Peel off the cheesecloth.

Decorate the cake with candied fruit and whole almonds.

The two sides of Easter

Age range
Nine upwards.

Group size
Individuals or whole class

What you need
Clay or Plasticine, or paper and paint or pastel crayons.

What to do
Discuss with the children the two aspects of Easter; the sadness of the events of Good Friday and the joy of the resurrection of Jesus on Easter Day. Talk about the items associated with each: the cross, purple cloth, tomb with stone across, broken bread, cup of wine, the empty cross, gold/white cloth, empty tomb with stone rolled away, communion wafers and flowers.

Now ask them to create appropriate pictures or models to portray both aspects. (See *Bright Ideas Easter Activities* for numerous other activities.)

85

Summer term

April Fool's Day

The reason for 1 April being 'All Fool's Day' is uncertain although one theory is that it relates to the French decree in 1564 that New Year began on 1 January as opposed to the end of March or the beginning of April. New Year gifts and messages were now given on 1 January but joke gifts and messages were given on 1 April as a memory of the times when 1 April was New Year's Day.

Another suggestion is that 1 April might have been the last day of festivities in the days when the New Year began on 25 March.

It is certainly a time when some spectacular spoofs have been known, including the nineteenth century invitation to the 'washing of the white lions' at the Tower of London and more recently there have been some television presentations of a tongue in cheek nature.

All teachers know the usual tricks of the day but are still caught out sometimes. Why not devise a trick to fool your class?

April fool trick

Age range
Nine plus.

Group size
Whole class.

What you need
The co-operation of two or more teachers and the headteacher.

What to do
The class teacher receives a note allegedly from the head. This note is relayed to the class and tells them about re-arrangements of their school day from the following Monday. It could state that the school day – and thus all breaks, including lunch time are changed to start one hour earlier. The end of the day however will be later for some apparently logical reason and the children are required to copy the new routines carefully from the blackboard to give to their parents. An air of authenticity may be ensured by a co-operative head or senior teacher popping into the classroom to confirm, with suitable gravity, the importance of the information.

Embellishments to this information might suggest that urgent new requirements are for a one hour compulsory 'homework period' at the end of the day.

April fool's boxes

Age range
Seven plus.

Group size
Individuals.

What you need
Small boxes (take-away individual burger boxes are ideal), coloured paper, felt-tipped pens or crayons, scissors, adhesive, sticky tape.

What to do
Each person will need to cut two strips of paper in contrasting colours about 4 cm wide and 50 cm long. These strips are placed at right angles to each other and the underneath strip folded around and over the top strip, keeping the two at right angles. This process is repeated for the whole length of the strips. The ends are then taped together to stop the strips unfolding.

A 'fool' jester head is then made from the coloured paper and stuck to one end flap of the folded strip. The other end of the strip is stuck to the bottom inside of the box. When the lid is closed the 'fool' should disappear inside the box.

The 'present' can then be given to a member of another class or one of the family who will get a surprise on opening it.

The children may like to make 'speech bubbles' saying 'April fool' and stick them to the jester's mouth so that they will be revealed when he pops out.

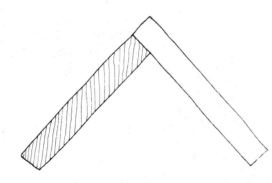

Fool's spelling test

Age range
Eight plus.

Group size
Whole class.

What you need
Paper, pencils, dictionaries.

What to do
Ask the children to find the deliberate mistakes in the following passage:

Today is April Fouls Day.
It is sprng and the twolips are coming out.
The dafudils are blooming.
Their wilt soon be lot more new flours.
Theya re coming out because of the sonshine.
The Eastar hollidays are next weak.
You will have some choclate eggs.
Maybe you can help with the gardenning.
Have some sandwitches on your picnick.
How menny missteakes did you find?

Ask the children to circle all the mistakes and then try to find the correct spelling for the 'fool' words.

Hans Andersen's Day

Hans Christian Andersen was born on 2 April 1805 and his birthday is celebrated in many countries. You could celebrate his special day or make it the start of a whole festival of books and story telling.

Young Hans was interested in acting and stories as a child. He was a clumsy boy, ugly and ungainly. When his father died he worked in a factory but eventually left to try the theatre. This was a failure and he was constantly told he was useless so he decided to write stories. Later, he remembered the stories told to him by his grandmother and he begn to write about the fantasy world of children. His stories made him famous throughout the world, almost a reflection of his own story was one called 'The Ugly Duckling' and now the *Fairy Tales of Hans Christian Andersen* has become a classic collection.

'The Ugly Duckling' story

Age range
Nine plus.

Group size
Individuals or whole class.

What you need
Copy of 'The Ugly Duckling' story,
paper,
pencils.

What to do
Read and then discuss the implications of the story. Then ask the children to re-write the story in other terms, from the point of view of a young child who seems to have little talent and then discovers that he has some very special ability of which others are envious, for instance.

Variation
Discuss the qualities and abilities the children feel that they would like to have. They could write about what having that talent or quality would mean and how they think they would use it.

A very important point which could be made from this story would be the importance of individuals being recognised as such and valued for the qualities they have. This could be developed as an exercise in which the children list their own strengths and weaknesses as a self-evaluation.

Younger children could act out 'The Ugly Duckling' story, perhaps using puppets and present it to the school at a special 'Hans Andersen' assembly.

World Health Day

World Health Day falls on 7 April. Many activities could be considered for a celebration of this day but one obvious starting point is a look at 'self' or 'me'; another is the idea of illness and disease.

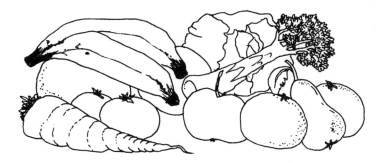

A look at what I eat

Age range
Seven plus.

Group size
Individuals or whole class.

What you need
Pencils, paper, copies of food diary (see page 127).

What to do
First have a general discussion with the class on what they have to eat at various meals, what snacks they eat, and what they drink. What do they think is a healthy diet?

Ask them to fill in the diary sheets over a week and then think about these questions in relation to what they have eaten over that week. Is their diet healthy?

Ask them to look at it in terms of food groups ie carbohydrates, proteins, fats, vitamins, minerals etc. What do we mean by a balanced diet? What are the essential nutrients? How could they improve their daily diet?

Now ask them to make charts showing these essential nutrients and to think about:

● Where can each one be found?
● What does it do for the body?

Variation
Ask the children to think about when they have felt hungry; perhaps they've been out and got home very late for a meal; during Ramadan, or when on a special diet for instance. Then ask them to consider the hunger felt by a large number of people, half the world's population, compared to the other half of the people who have more than they need. What causes hunger? Can they think of ways they could help?

Illness
Ask the children to think about the meaning of illness and being unwell, the idea of not functioning normally, of being 'off colour' and the possible reasons for this. They could consider and write about:
'Healthy habits' – ways in which illness can be prevented: diet, body care etc. The class could produce a book called 'Health is . . .' In this the children should write their own definitions of good health or their view of the value of good health.

Baisakhi

Baisakhi is the name of the first month in the Indian year and Baisakhi day is celebrated on 13 April so it is the beginning of a new year. It is an old Indian festival celebrated all over India but it is especially important to Sikhs. On this day they remember how in 1699 on Baisakhi Day, Guru Gobind Singh formed the brotherhood of the Khalsa. It marked the beginning of a new phase in the Sikh religion, the day when the Sikhs became a strong, military brotherhood who swore loyalty to their faith and promised to defend the weak.

The festival lasts for three days, two of which are spent reading the *Guru Granth Sahib*, the Sikh Holy Book. On the third day, those who want to join the fellowship of the Khalsa go through the ceremony which brings them into it. They drink a special kind of sugared water called amrit, and recieve the five Ks:

Kesh – uncut hair;
Kangha – the comb fixed in the hair;
Kara – the steel bracelet worn on the right wrist;
Kirpan – the short sword;
Kaccha – the shorts.
The turban and these five articles constitute a uniform which all Sikhs wear.

The congregation gathers for prayers and hymns and the sharing of fruit and Karah Prasad (ghee, flour, milk and sugar). After the ceremony they go to the **Langar** for a vegetarian meal.

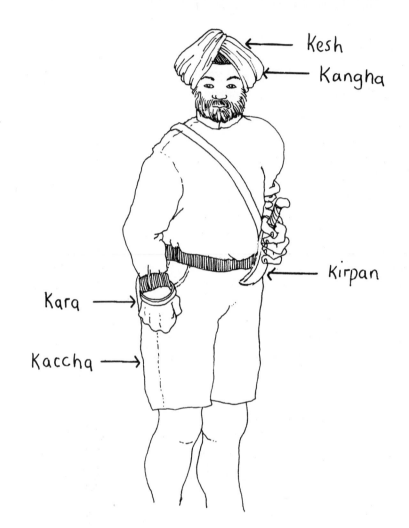

Kesh

Kangha

Kirpan

Kara

Kaccha

The five Ks

Age range
Seven plus.

Group size
Individuals.

What you need
Paper, pens or crayons, pencils.

What to do
First collect some pictures of men and women wearing different kinds of uniforms and see if you and the children can find out the meanings behind these uniforms – are they symbolic or historical for example? Which of these reasons seem to be important to those who belong to the Sikh Khalsa?

Then ask the children to make pictures of a Sikh person wearing the five Ks. They should label these when finished with a short explanation of each symbol.

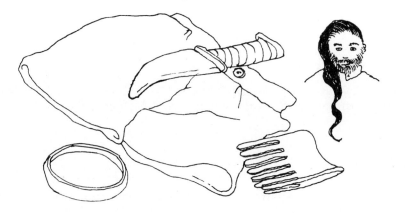

Other initiation ceremonies

Age range
Nine plus.

Group size
Individuals and small groups.

What you need
Reference books on main religions would be helpful, paper, pencils, pens or coloured pencils.

What to do
Ask the children to think of other ceremonies of initiation, the clothes or badges worn and any special actions which are performed or promises made. They could find out about: the Bar Mitzvah of Jewish boys, confirmation in the Anglican and Roman Catholic churches, becoming a monk or becoming enrolled in the Guides or Scouts, for example.

Are there any changes which are believed to happen to a person undergoing the ceremony?

After they have done their research, the children can work in small groups to produce some kind of permanent means of recording what they have found out. This could be narrative, annotated pictures, a diary written by a person undergoing the ceremony, a tape recording, or even a model.

St George's Day

St George is the patron saint of England and also of soldiers and 23 April is his special saint's day.

Very little is actually known about St George but it is possible that he was a Roman soldier who was martyred by the emperor for being a Christian. There are many references to St George overcoming evil. Many years ago evil was considered to take several forms — hence the notion of the dragon which was one these forms of evil. The story of St George and the dragon is well-established folklore and the image of the brave knight fighting the evil of the dragon to save the beautiful princess is equally well known.

St George's flag is a red cross on a white background and can be seen flying above many public buildings and parish churches on 23 April. His day was declared a public holiday in 1222 but is no longer so.

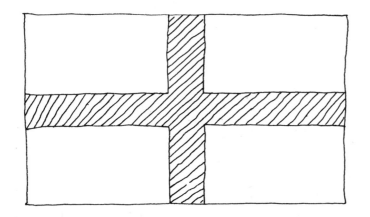

(This day is also the birthday of William Shakespeare and the occasion is always celebrated in his home town, Stratford-upon-Avon, Warwickshire.)

St George's shield

Age range
Seven plus.

Group size
Individuals.

What you need
Template for a shield outline, felt-tipped pens, pencils, paints.

What to do
Ask the children to design an emblem for the shield, using one or more of the following: a rose, a red cross, a dragon.

Variation
The children could make more permanent shields using plywood cut on a shaper saw or fret saw, and painted with PVA paint, which can be varnished when dry.

Ramadan

People who follow the religion of Islam, Muslims, live out their lives according to the teaching of the prophet, Muhammad, who lived about 1400 years ago. He taught them to believe in Allah and to submit to his will. Ramadan is a reminder of the discipline that this requires and during the month called Ramadan, Muslims get up before dawn and eat breakfast. They then have no more food or drink from sunrise to sunset. The *Qur'an* says that the fast must begin from the time there is sufficient light to distinguish a black thread from a white one. Children under ten are not expected to fast.

During Ramadan, Muslims make extra efforts in religious matters and many spend a lot of time at the mosque. The end of Ramadan is a time of happiness and on the last night of Ramadan when a new moon is expected people crowd the streets watching the sky for the sign that Ramadan is over.

The first day of the new month is celebrated as Eid ul-Fitr, the festival of fast breaking. (At present, this is in May). The fast is broken, often by eating a date. There is a dawn prayer at the mosque followed by Zakat ul-Fitr – offerings of money to charity, the festival prayers and then a special breakfast.

After breakfast families call on one another and new clothes are important for this occasion. People take gifts of sweets and sugared almonds in decorated boxes to give to friends and children are given sweets, nuts and money. Many Muslims send Eid cards to each other and these bear the greeting 'Eid Mubarak'.

Make an Eid card

Age range
Six plus.

Group size
Individuals.

What you need
Thin card, coloured papers, foils, adhesive, felt-tipped pens, scissors.

What to do
The children must be reminded that the Islamic religion forbids making pictures of living things, but flowers, patterns and minarets are appropriate items for the cards. Let the children work out their own designs but tell them that Eid cards will need to open the opposite way from the cards we send at Christmas etc. The greeting is often 'Eid Mubarak' and is written thus:

Islamic patterns

Age range
Six plus.

Group size
Pairs.

What you need
Geometric shapes,
triangles,
hexagons,
squares etc,
paper,
pencils,
pens,
coloured sticky paper,
scissors.

What to do
Get the children to experiment with the shapes, seeing which will tessellate and designing a variety of patterns. They can then begin to build up patterns on paper, first drawing round the shapes and when the design is complete, they can be coloured in with pens. They can also make some patterns by drawing around the shapes on to the sticky paper and building up symmetrical patterns.

Variation
Small groups could work together to make sheets of 'snap cards' based on Islamic patterns. Remind the children that the Islamic religion forbids the representation of living things in pictures, so their cards must not show such things as kings and queens. Patterns based on flower or plant forms are acceptable as are those based on geometric designs.

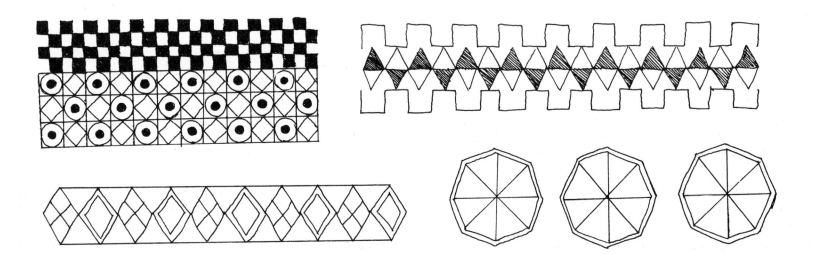

Semolina halva

Age range
Five to eleven.

Groups size
Small groups with adult supervision.

What you need
Saucepan, wooden spoon, shallow dish.

Ingredients
50 g butter,
seeds of two cardamoms white or green,
125 g semolina,
125 g granulated sugar,
450 ml hot water,
chopped almonds,
sultanas.

What to do
Melt the butter with the cardamom seeds in a saucepan (the butter must NOT brown). Add the semolina and cook gently until the mixture turns golden. Remove from heat.

Add the sugar and water and bring the mixture to the boil, stirring all the time. Gently simmer until the mixture is of a thick consistency, stirring occasionally to prevent burning.

Pour the halva into a buttered dish and decorate with nuts and sultanas.

Making sevian

Age range
Five to eleven.

Group size
Small groups with adult supervision.

What you need
Saucepan, wooden spoon, shallow dish.

Ingredients
1 litre milk,
100 g sugar,
2 cardamom pods,
100 g vermicelli,
chopped nuts or cinnamon.

What to do
Boil down the milk until it has reduced by half and thickened. Add the sugar and cardamom pods.

When the mixture is creamy, add the vermicelli and simmer until the vermicelli is soft and the mixture is thick and creamy.

Remove the cardamom pods. Sprinkle with chopped nuts or cinnamon. Sevian can be served warm or chilled.

May Day

This is celebrated on 1 May. The earliest celebrations of May Day seem to be connected with pagan ritual, probably in the Roman festival honouring Maia, mother of Mercury, on the first day of her month. There were sacrifices and considerable merry-making related to this festival.

Celtic tradition honoured the first day of May as 'Beltane', the first day of summer and bonfires proliferated, perhaps as a means of helping the sun regain its power to warm and encourage growth and fruition. It was also the day when cattle were taken back to the upland pastures, having been brought down from the hills in November.

In the fourteenth and fifteenth centuries May Day was a public holiday with considerable fun and it was sometimes viewed with concern by the Church for the excesses which were associated with the festival. Traditionally the day was characterised by garlands, pretty dresses and a general rest from work. Customs such as Maypole dancing and crowning the May Queen developed, and for many years there has been the association of 1 May as Labour Day with public celebrations, rallies and parades all over the world.

May Day crown

Age range
Six to nine.

Group size
Individuals.

What you need
Card strips approximately 8 cm wide, tissue-paper in various colours, paper saucers or circles cut from card, scissors, adhesive, stapler.

What to do
Cut the card to fit the head and staple the ends in place. Stick the saucers around the crown.

Make flowers from the coloured tissue-paper and stick them on to the circles and the card strip in a formal pattern.

May Day baskets

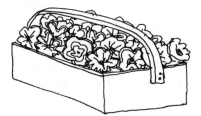

Age range
Six to eleven.

Group size
Individuals.

What you need
Rectangular pieces of thin card or paper approximately A4 size, adhesive or stapler, thin strips of paper or card, assorted tissue-paper and coloured paper, scissors.

What to do
Each child will need one sheet of card and a strip for the handle; first draw a line all round the sheet about 4 cm from the edge to form a rectangle. Then fold in from each side towards the middle:

fold along dotted lines

Open out and cut along solid lines:

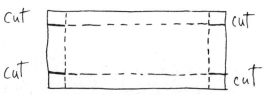

cut   cut

cut   cut

Bring the sides and the ends up along the folds. Now bend in the end flaps and stick or staple at the corners. Finally staple or stick the handle in place. The children can then make paper flowers to be placed inside their baskets. These can be stuck in place as they are made.

Japanese Boys' Day

Japanese Boys' Day or Tangonosekku is a traditional holiday celebrated on 5 May which honours boys in Japan. In more recent years, however, Japan had designated 5 May as Children's Day (Kodomonohi). Carp kites are flown from bamboo flagpoles in people's gardens; one kite for each son, the oldest son normally having the largest, most beautiful kite. Boys are encouraged to be strong and brave like the carp that struggles upstream.

Fragrant iris leaves are often put in a boy's evening bath water by the mother; the sword-shaped iris leaf being symbolic of the spirit of brave warriors. A display of Samurai warrior dolls is often made and if the family has any armour, this is also displayed.

Make a tilting doll

Age range
Six to eleven.

Group size
Individuals.

What you need
Balloons, wallpaper paste, newspaper, seeds or rice, paint, varnish, Japanese pictures if possible.

What to do
Ask the children to blow up their balloons and tie a knot. To make the papier mâché soak strips of newspaper in wallpaper paste and add a layer at time. Make the layers even and leave a small hole at the top. Leave the covered balloon to dry completely. When it is dry burst the balloon.

Now the 'doll' needs to be filled: add the rice or seeds through the hole at the top. The children will need to experiment here so that the doll will return to a standing

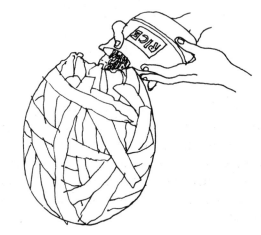

position when pushed gently. When this has been achieved, cover the hole with papier mâché, and leave to dry. When thoroughly dry, the doll can be decorated. If possible show the children pictures of Japanese Samurai warriors; these can be helpful when they decorate the doll, and add the features.

When the dolls have all been finished the children could hold a mock battle ie whose doll will keep rocking the most time? This could be done in the form of a knockout competition or each person could count the number of 'rocks' for their own doll. Why not ask the children for suggestions as to how to hold the battle and record the results.

Iris paintings

Age range
Five to eleven.

Group size
Individuals.

What you need
Paints, brushes, palettes, pens, iris flowers, charcoal.

What to do
Talk with the children about the shapes and colours they can see in the flowers; they should notice the markings on the petals particularly. Some may wish to sketch the shapes in charcoal.

They can then try to paint the flowers as accurately as possible, taking care to mix their paints as near as they can to the colours of the flowers. When dry, markings can be added, either with very fine brushes, or pens.

Write a haiku

Age range
Eight plus.

Group size
Individuals.

What you need
Paper, pencils, examples of Japanese haiku.

What to do
Read the children some examples of the form and explain what haiku is: a form of Japanese poetry, unrhymed and consisting of three lines written in a five-seven-five syllabic pattern, usually on the subject of nature and its seasonal aspects.

For children who are not familiar with the notion of syllables you could use their names as an introduction to the idea before embarking on this activity.

Now ask the children to try to write their own haiku possibly on the subject of irises in spring/summer.

Wesak

Wesak is a Buddist festival, sometimes called Visakha Puja. It takes place on the full moon day of the month of Visakha, usually in May or June. It is a time when Buddists celebrate the birth, enlightenment and death of the Buddha (all of which occurred on the same day but in different years!). Of the two main groups of Buddhists, it is those of the Theravadan school who live mainly in Sri Lanka, Burma, and Thailand who celebrate all three events on the same day.

A large puja is held as Wesak is most importantly a time of worship. The temples and homes are decorated with lanterns and flowers and offerings of flowers are placed in front of the statues of the Buddha. In the evening, processions go around the temple with burning incense sticks and candles and during the night a sermon takes place telling of the great teachings of the Buddha.

Extra generosity and hospitality is shown to the monks at Wesak and sometimes captured birds or fish are freed to demonstrate the compassion and love of the Buddha.

Flower garlands

Age range
Five plus.

Group size
Individuals or pairs.

What you need
Coloured tissue-paper circles (you may wish to pre-cut these for the youngest children), paper adhesive, wool or thread, scissors, large needles.

What to do
Make tissue-paper flowers, using two circles for each one; these can be both of one colour or contrasting colours. Place a small dot of adhesive in the centre of one circle, put the other circle on top and twist the two together slightly from the centre back. When the adhesive has dried, the flowers can be strung on the thread using the large blunt needle. The children will need to leave sufficient thread at each end so that the garland can be tied.

The important things in life

Age range
Seven plus.

Group size
Individuals and whole class.

What you need
Pencils, paper.

What to do
Talk with the children about what they consider the most important things in life. They can then each compile a list of ten things which they consider to be most important. After this has been done, see what individuals have suggested and then come up with one list of ten items chosen from those on all the lists.

Now ask everyone to put this list in order, starting with the most important. This will receive ten points, the second choice nine points, and so on. At the end of the activity go round the class and find out how many points each person has given to each of the items on the list. A pair of children can then work out the totals and see which item is considered the most important by the group, and which least important. How does this compare with the individual's lists?

Kindness to animals book

Age range
Seven plus.

Group size
Small groups.

What you need
Rough paper, pencils, coloured pens, crayons etc, thin card or strong paper, card.

What to do
Remind the children that the Buddha taught that we should be kind to animals, and that birds and fish are sometimes set free at Wesak. Ask them to work together in their groups to produce books for younger children which should encourage them to take care of animals. They may like to centre on care of pets, or conservation for instance.

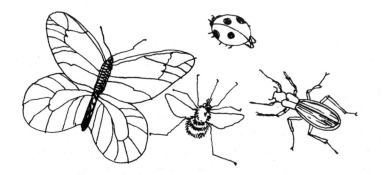

After drafts have been worked on, and the books themselves produced, the groups will need to work on the covers. Discuss with them the kind of information that should be put on a cover; author, illustrator, publisher, a little about the story and its makers etc.

Some of these could also be shared at a Wesak assembly. If you do plan to hold a special Wesak assembly, a group of children could work on a large mural depicting an aspect of the life of Siddhartha, the Buddha.

An appropriate poem for such an assembly would be Christina Rossetti's 'Hurt no living thing':

Hurt no living thing:
  Ladybird, nor butterfly,
Nor moth with dusty wing,
  Nor cricket chirping cheerily,
Nor grasshopper so light of leap,
  Nor dancing gnat, nor beetle fat,
Nor harmless worms that creep.

World Environment Day

World Environment Day falls on 5 June and this should be a day when we think about preserving and enhancing the environment. A good place to start is the school playground or field.

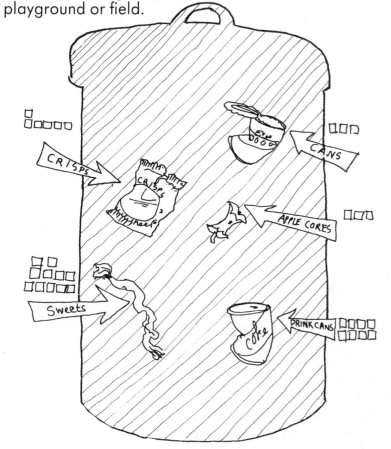

Litter hunt

Age range
Six plus.

Group size
Small groups.

What you need
Plastic sacks or carrier bags, newspaper, grey paper strips or coloured sugar paper, rubber gloves (optional).

What to do
Direct the children to specific areas of the playground or field where they should pick up all items of litter (not broken glass) and collect it in their sacks. Take the rubbish inside and empty sacks on to newspaper to see what has been collected. You may want the children to wear rubber gloves for this activity.

Results can be displayed by cutting out a large dustbin shape from the grey paper. The children can cut paper arrows for each group of items – tins, crisp bags, tissues etc and the item written on the arrow. Separate small squares of paper can indicate the number of each item and these can be stuck above the arrows which are added to the display pointing into the dustbin. An example of each item can be fixed to the dustbin shape.

Follow-up
The children will probably be concerned about the amount of rubbish found and could then make posters encouraging others to 'keep our school playground clean'. These can be prominently displayed around the school. After a week, hold another litter search and see if there has been any improvement. If there has, change the numbers on the item arrows on the display.

Save our environment book

Age range
Seven plus.

Group size
Pairs and whole class.

What you need
Paper, pens, crayons, magazines, adhesive, scissors.

What to do
Have a general discussion with the class about ways that people spoil the environment – litter, smoke from factories, cigarettes, car fumes, killing animals for furs, the use of weedkillers etc. Try to encourage them to think of their own ideas.

If you have a copy of *Dinosaurs and All That Rubbish*, Michael Foreman (Picture Puffin), sharing the story will provide an exciting starting point or extension to the activity.

After the discussion the children can work in pairs, each pair taking one aspect of the discussion and making a page for a class book on the theme 'Don't spoil our environment' – let the children decide on the title. They can either draw or hunt through magazines to find illustrations for their page.

Dragon boat festival

This is a Chinese festival which usually falls in June and commemorates the poet statesman, Ch'u Yuen, who is supposed to have thrown himself from a cliff and drowned himself in a lake rather than agree to the emperor's policies. So popular was he with the people that they are said to have thrown lumps of rice in, and created as much noise as possible to divert the marauding demons and fish so that his body would not be eaten.

In China local villages and towns hold boat races and the boats often have a dragon head carved on the front. Rice is a speciality of this festival and people often eat rice dumplings wrapped in leaves.

Dragon boats

Age range
Six to eleven.

Group size
Individuals.

What you need
Empty juice or milk cartons (make sure they are clean), stapler, scissors, a variety of coloured papers, crayons or pens.

What to do
The children should draw a dragon's head on their coloured paper, adding whatever features they wish. (Let them work out the appropriate size for this head bearing in mind that it will be attached to the carton.) Cut out the shape of the head.

They should then staple the top of the carton closed and place it on its side (horizontally). The upper part of the carton should then be cut away (see diagram).

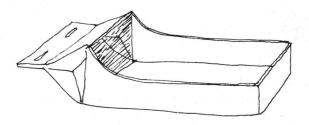

The dragon head is then stapled to the upper, slanted part of the carton.

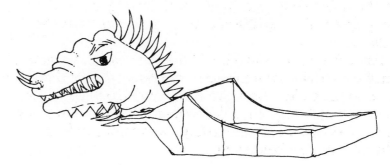

Flag Day and American Independence Day

Flag Day falls on 14 June and is to commemorate that day in 1777 when Congress adopted the flag with 13 alternate stripes of white and red, representing the 13 original states and the union represented by 13 white stars on a blue background. As each state was adopted another star was added to the field of blue and there are now 50 altogether (including Alaska and Hawaii).

Independence Day is celebrated on 4 July and is a national holiday in the USA. It commemorates 4 July 1776, the signing of the Declaration of Independence. This declaration was signed in Independence Hall, Pennsylvania, and is on display there for everyone to see.

American word book

Age range
Seven plus.

Group size
Individuals and whole class.

What you need
Paper, pencils, thick paper for zig-zag book, pens.

What to do
Ask the children to think of and write down as many words as they can for which they know the American equivalent. You may help them by providing a few American words such as 'sidewalk' and 'cookies' as a start. When everyone has made as full a list as possible, have a class discussion to see what the children have written.

Then individuals can take turns to add one of their items to a class zig-zag book. They should put in both the American word, its English equivalent and a small picture. To make it more demanding you may want to ask them to make the book in alphabetical order like a dictionary, in which case this will have to be worked out beforehand, possibly by a small committee who must also decide which word will come first, the American or the English.

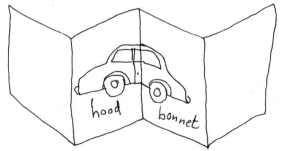

Chalk stars and stripes pattern

Age range
Seven to eleven.

Group size
Individuals.

What you need
Large sheets of white sugar paper, pencils, red and blue chalk, scissors, small squares of paper approximately 8 cm × 8 cm, strip of paper the same length as the large sheet.

What to do
The children should first cut out a star shape like the one shown. They should then draw around this on the small square of paper. Then, leaving the border intact, they should cut out the star shape from the middle of the square.

The next step is to chalk heavily around the edges of the star stencil. The chalked stencil is then placed on the large sheet of paper and held firmly in place with one hand. The fingers of the other hand are pushed across the chalked edges on to the paper underneath. This is done around the whole star shape and the stencil removed to reveal a star.

If the stencil is re-chalked and moved, another star shape can be made and so on, to form a pattern.

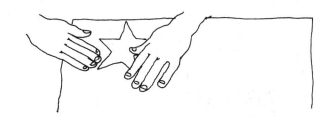

To make the stripes the edge of the paper strip is chalked and the same process is used as for the stars.

Encourage the children to experiment with different patterns. (Those they want to preserve can be sprayed with chalk fixative.)

The templates can also be used for splatter painting, using a toothbrush charged with thick paint.

Waldorf salad

Age range
Five plus.

Group size
Small group with adult supervision.

What you need
Chopping board, sharp knife for cutting, large bowl.

Ingredients
3 red apples,
4 celery sticks,
25 g walnuts,
125 ml mayonnaise,
1 orange
1 small lettuce.

What to do
Explain to the children that this salad is named after a famous hotel in New York.

Cut the apples (unpeeled) into quarters and remove the cores; then cut into smaller pieces. Slice celery, cutting at a slight diagonal across the stems; chop walnuts (keep back a few unchopped). Place all the ingredients into a bowl and mix with the mayonnaise.

Peel the orange, remove pith and break into segments. Spread lettuce leaves on serving dish and pile the apple mixture in the centre. Decorate with orange segments and a few walnuts.

Blueberry muffins

Age range
Six plus.

Group size
Small group with adult supervision.

What you need
Bun tin (a baking tray with paper cake-cases will do), mixing bowl, sieve, fork, small bowl, saucepan, wooden spoon, teaspoon.

Ingredients
50 g sugar,   1 egg,
200 g plain flour,   225 ml milk,
2 tsps baking powder,   50 g melted margarine.
pinch of salt,   100 g blueberries.
(Blueberries are obtainable in Britain but they are rather expensive; try frozen. Alternatively use blackberries, frozen will do.)

What to do
Set oven to 425°F/220°C/gas mark 7.

Grease the bun tin or set out cake cases on a baking tray. Sieve the sugar, flour, baking powder and salt into a bowl. Beat the egg in another bowl and add the milk and melted margarine. Mix well. Add the washed berries to the flour and mix. Make a well in the centre of the flour and pour in the egg mixture. Mix up with wooden spoon, stirring the flour from the sides into the liquid in the centre. Continue until the dry ingredients are moistened. Fill sections of the bun tin or cake cases about two thirds full. Put in the oven and bake for about 20-25 minutes until the muffins are puffed up and golden brown in colour.

They are best eaten hot from the oven.

Design and make a class flag

Age range
Seven plus.

Group size
Individuals and whole class.

What you need
Paper, pens or crayons, large piece of plain fabric about 120 cm × 65 cm, fabric offcuts, needles, sewing thread, cardboard, safety pins, adhesive.

What to do
First ask the children to make their own designs for a class flag. They will need to to be able to explain why they have chosen the particular symbols and colours they have used. When all these are finished, get the class together to decide which symbols and colours are to be incorporated into the flag.

Now appoint a design committee who have to work out a layout. Another committee can then transfer this layout on to the large piece of fabric. Pin the different parts of the design and stitch on to the flag with either a running or blanket stitch.

The finished flag can be hung in a conspicuous place in the classroom.

Why not try to involve the whole school by asking each class to design and make its own flag. These can be hung outside each class.

The design could then be made into class badges, using small pieces of thick card, coloured pens, safety pins (or masking tape) and adhesive. They could be laminated with self-adhesive book covering.

design it

make it

display it

make badges

St Swithun's Day

St Swithun's Day falls on 15 July and it is said that if it rains on that day it is likely to be wet for the next 40 days:

St Swithun's Day, if thou dost rain,
For forty days it will remain.
St Swithun's Day, if thou be fair,
For forty days 'twill rain no more.

The old wives tale is based on something that happened in the ninth century.

St Swithun, a much loved Bishop of Winchester, who disliked pomp and show, requested of the church that when he died he should be buried outside the cathedral so that all who came to worship could walk on his grave. His wish was granted but only for a while. His body was later moved by monks into Winchester Cathedral itself, and it was supposed to have rained for 40 days, the assumption being that St Swithun was showing his disapproval.

When it does rain on 15 July, country people often say that St Swithun is 'christening the apples'.

Weather lore watch

Age range
Six plus.

Group size
Individuals and whole class.

What you need
Paper, pens, pencils, crayons, books about the countryside.

What to do
Tell the children that in country lore, some plants and animals are used to show the weather, when it is going to rain for instance. Explain that they are not reliable necessarily but suggest that they watch out for the signs and see if they were right. Also suggest that they look in books and ask other people if they know any weather lore.

Here are some examples of weather lore:

- Rooks gather near their rookeries when rain clouds appear.
- Cattle and horses gather on the leeward side (away from the wind) of hedges when rain is coming.
- Cattle often lie down in the fields before rain.
- Pine cones close up before rain.

Individuals can collect examples and all these can be put together in a class book along with any observations which the children may be able to make on the accuracy or otherwise of the unofficial weather forecasts.

They can also study cloud patterns to see if these have any connection with the weather. Do different clouds produce different kinds of rain?

Rainy-day board game

Age range
Six to eleven.

Group size
Small groups.

What you need
Rough paper, pencils, felt-tipped pens, large sheets of card (approximately A3 size), dice and shaker.

What to do
Working in their groups the children will need to plan out a layout for their game, based on a rainy day. It could be going to school, going shopping or any other appropriate activity in the rain.

They will need to devise a number of hazards such as 'Umbrella turns inside out' – 'Miss two turns'; 'Step in a puddle' – 'Go back two squares' etc and some bonuses 'Friend gives a lift to bus stop' – 'Have another turn' for example.

Once the game has been made, they can try playing it with the others in the group initially and then you could arrange a game swap.

If you want the children to make their own dice and counters you could provide some small wooden cubes to which they could add symbols such as boots, a raindrop etc and these can be made to denote number symbols. In this case, the makers will need to provide a key. Counters could be made from a quick hardening clay – wellington shapes for example, would be suitable.

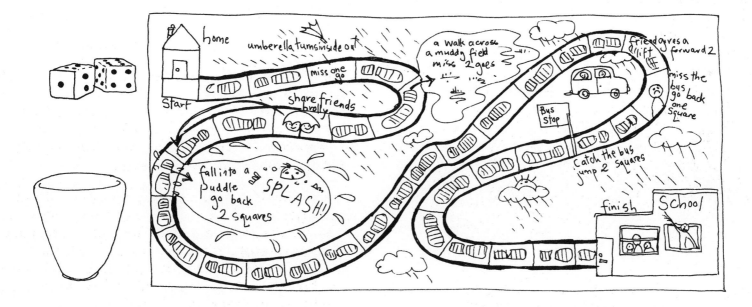

Raksha Bandhan

Raksha Bandhan is a Hindu festival and is also celebrated by many Sikh families. It takes place in July or August and is a day on which sisters honour their brothers, who in turn offer protection to their sisters. Raksha Bandhan means 'ties of protection' and on this day sisters tie a band of thread around their brothers' wrists. The band is called a rakhi and is a sign of love and a plea for protection. In addition the girl marks her brother's forehead with red powder. Another festival is also celebrated on this day – the Day of Coconuts and sometimes families will combine the two festivals.

There are many stories associated with Raksha Bandhan, one of which tells how Indra, king of the lesser gods lost his kingdom to a demon, Bali, in a war. Indra's wife, Sacha Devi, sought the help of Lord Vishnu. The god gave her a thread – an amulet – to tie around her husband's right wrist before he went into battle with the demon king. Indra is said to have won back his kingdom by virtue of this amulet.

Coconut Day, Nariyal Purnima, marks the end of the rainy season when fishermen in particular invoke Varuna, the sea god with offerings of coconuts. Coconuts are considered to be sacred.

Make a rakhi

Age range
Six plus.

Group size
Individuals.

What you need
Wool or thick thread or ribbon in contrasting colours, red and yellow especially, scissors.

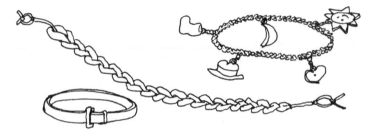

What to do
The children will need to decide whom they are making the rakhi for – it may be a brother, or a friend if they don't have a brother. They will need to know how long to make the band. (If the brother is not available at school, they will need to have measured his wrist beforehand.) They can then either plait the two colours together or twist them in some way. The ends can be fastened by tying a piece of cotton around each to prevent the plaiting from coming undone.

At the same time you can ask your class to make a collection of bangles and bracelets for a display. Are any of them of special significance such as the kara for instance; or perhaps some people may have identity bracelets given to them, at a christening for example.

Wrist measuring

Age range
Five plus.

Group size
Individuals or whole class.

What you need
Strips of thin paper or tape (string would do), scissors, large sheet of paper, preferably 1 cm squared for older children, adhesive or sticky tape.

What to do
Each child should measure around his right wrist with the tape or paper strip (younger children may need the help of a partner) and cut the appropriate length. There are various ways these can be displayed: the youngest children could sort them and mount them in order of length.

Older children who use standard units could measure their strips and then mount them in order. (If centimetre squared paper is used for mounting it may be a way of introducing the use of standard units to children who are at the appropriate stage of development.)

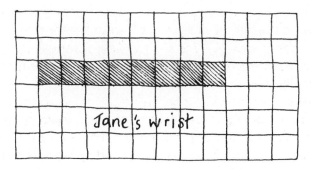

Brothers and sisters survey

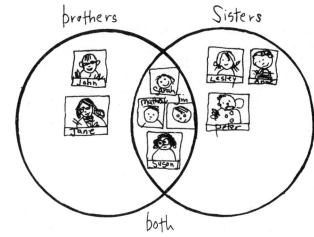

Age range
Five plus.

Group size
Whole class.

What you need
Paper, pens or crayons, scissors, large paper for mounting, sorting hoops – cut from paper, drawn or ready made.

What to do
Ask each member of the class to draw a picture of themselves on a piece of paper (approximately 10 cm × 10 cm). This is then cut out and the name attached. Make two sets: one for those who have brothers and one for those who have sisters – an intersection will be needed for those who have both. The children can then stick their picture on the appropriate part of the mounting paper. What about those who have no brother or sister – where will they go?

Making coconut barfi

Age range
Five plus.

Group size
Small groups with adult supervision.

What you need
Saucepan, wooden spoon, knife, baking tray.

Ingredients
175 g can evaporated milk,
100 g light brown sugar
(granulated),
75 g desiccated coconut.

What to do
Pour the evaporated milk into the saucepan and add the sugar. Heat gently stirring occasionally. Bring the mixture to the boil and simmer until the milk has reduced by about half its volume.

Stir in the desiccated coconut. Keep stirring until the mixture forms a sticky lump in the centre of the pan.

Remove the saucepan from the heat and spread the mixture on a greased metal tray. When cool cut into small cubes.

This recipe will make about 16-18 pieces. For a whole class you may wish to make two lots.

Janmashtami

This is a Hindu festival which falls on the eighth day of Shravan, which comes between July and September. It celebrates the birthday of Krishna, an incarnation of Vishnu, who fights against evil and loves life, so his birthday is a time of fun and happiness.

The real celebrations start at midnight, the time Krishna was born and up until that time of day, people fast. They come to the temple to see children acting out stories of Krishna or to hear stories about him. Just before midnight a statue of the infant Krishna is washed with ghee, yogurt, milk, sugar and honey. The mixture is collected and later shared with everyone and a statue or picture of the infant

is placed on a beautifully decorated swing which everyone can push. At midnight a ceremony is performed with a lamp, bells are rung and sweets are distributed. A feast is then held.

When the infant Krishna was born, he had to be smuggled out of the prison in which Devaki (his mother) and her husband were being kept by the demon Kansa. Kansa was planning to kill Krishna but his father managed to escape from the prison, taking the baby with him. Another baby, a special baby girl, was left in Krishna's place and when Kansa came to kill the child, the baby flew up into the air and told the wicked Kansa that Krishna was safe and would return to kill him some day.

Make a decorated swing

Age range
Seven plus.

Group size
Pairs.

What you need
Small cardboard boxes, pipe-cleaners, fabric scraps, coloured paper, tissue-paper in various colours, string or thread, adhesive, scissors, thick card.

What to do
Ask the children to construct a decorated swing from the junk materials supplied. Do not tell them exactly what to do but let them work out a means of making the cradle swing for themselves. They can use pipe-cleaners and fabric scraps to make the baby Krishna.

Reproducible material

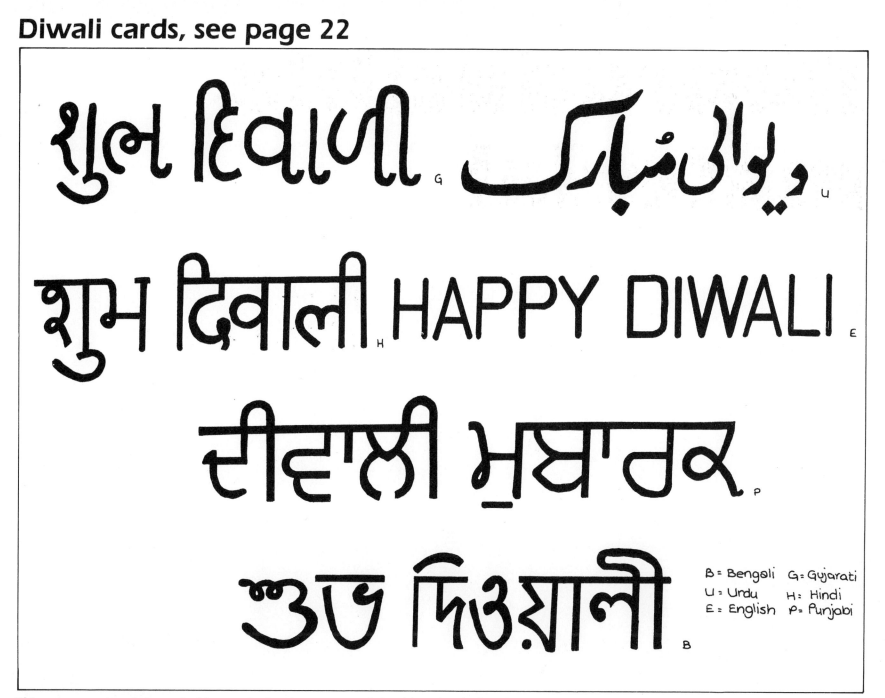

शुभ दिवाली G

ديوالی مبارک U

शुभ दिवाली H

HAPPY DIWALI E

दीवाली मुबारक P

শুভ দিওয়ালী B

B = Bengali G = Gujarati
U = Urdu H = Hindi
E = English P = Punjabi

Making dummy fireworks 1, see page 28

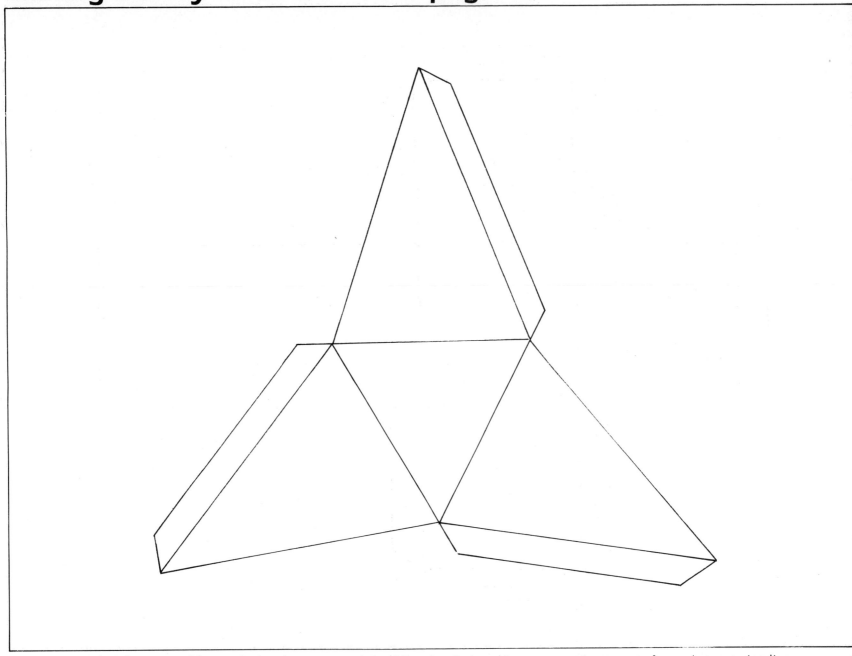

Dreidel to make, see page 35

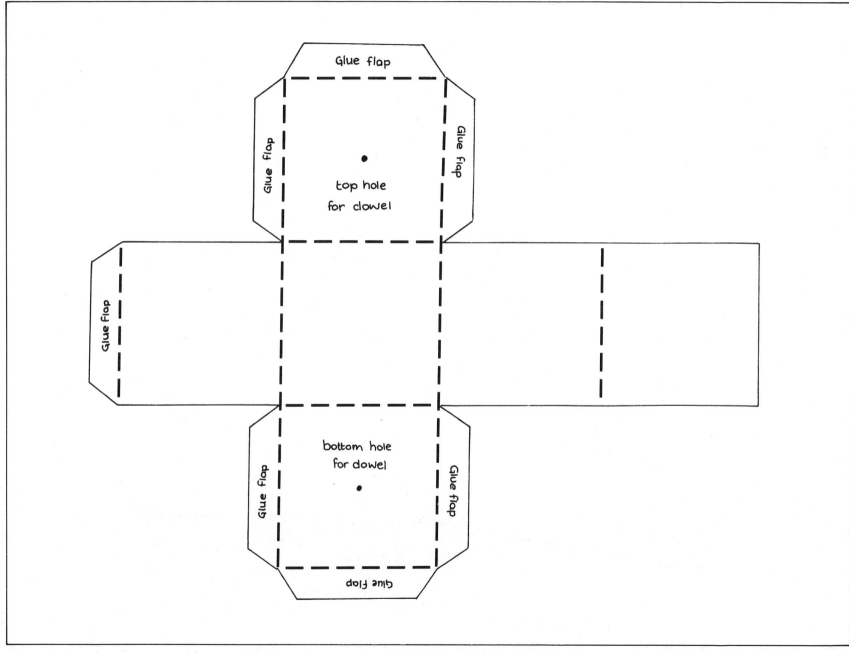

Menorah design, see page 38

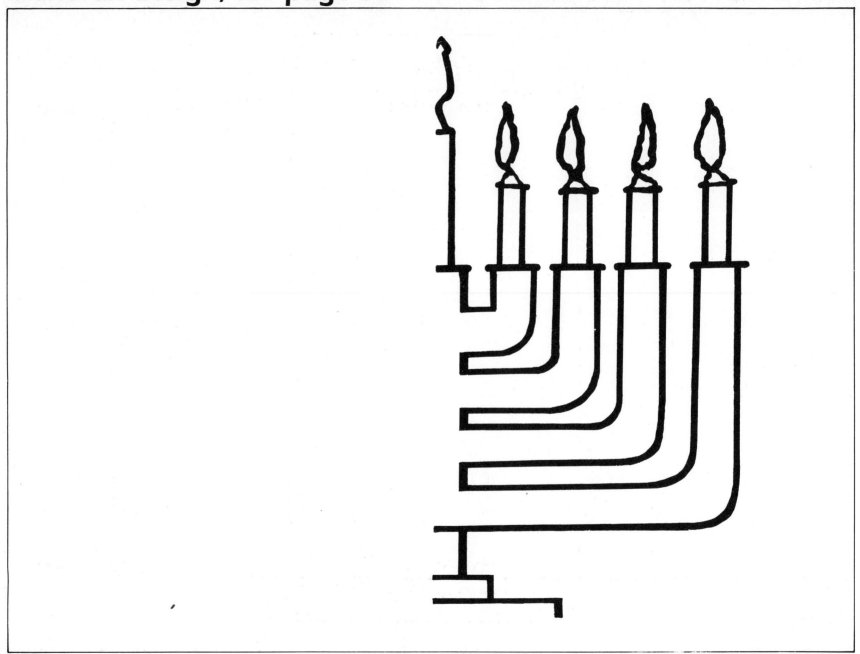

Lucky money envelope, see page 51

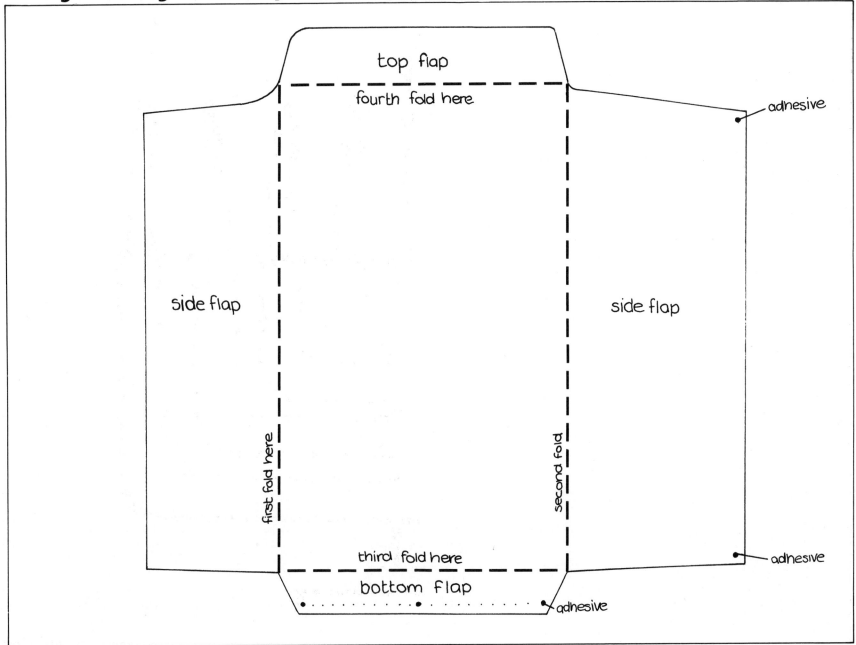

top flap

fourth fold here

adhesive

side flap

side flap

first fold here

second fold

third fold here

bottom flap

adhesive

adhesive

Chinese animal years, see page 54

Years of the rat: 1900, 1912, 1924, 1936, 1948, 1960, 1972, 1984. Rats tend to sleep all day and hunt at night. Those born during the day are likely to have easy lives; those born at night may have a life of hard work. People born in these years are usually cheerful and kind. They make friends easily. They are good at saving money.

Years of the ox: 1901, 1913, 1925, 1937, 1949, 1961, 1973, 1985. The ox is a strong, faithful animal. People born in these years are usually strong, quiet and good at using their hands. They tend to keep themselves to themselves and may be stubborn; others are warm and have lots of friends.

Years of the tiger: 1902, 1914, 1926, 1938, 1950, 1962, 1974, 1986. Those born in these years are often brave and powerful and intelligent. They are often leaders and do well in life. They may also be agile.

Years of the hare (or rabbit): 1903, 1915, 1927, 1939, 1951, 1963, 1975, 1987. People born in these years are usually lucky, happy and successful. They may have many children and are sometimes shy.

Years of the dragon: 1904, 1916, 1928, 1940, 1952, 1964, 1976, 1988. People born in these years are usually full of energy, healthy and like to do things on a grand scale. They are also very honest and need a purpose in life.

Years of the snake: 1905, 1917, 1929, 1941, 1953, 1965, 1977, 1989. People born in these years are usually wise and firm. They tend to be very careful about what they say, liking to think things over carefully. They can often become rich as they are shrewd over things of work.

Chinese animal years, see page 54

Years of the horse: 1906, 1918, 1930, 1942, 1954, 1966, 1978, 1990. A person born in these years is said to be popular, cheerful and quick-witted. On the other hand someone born in these years can be stubborn and impulsive.

Years of the ram (sheep or goat): 1907, 1919, 1931, 1943, 1955, 1967, 1979, 1991. The sheep is known for being gentle and compassionate. People born in these years also tend to be sincere, mild-mannered or shy. They are also inclined to worry.

Years of the monkey: 1908, 1920, 1932, 1944, 1956, 1968, 1980, 1992. People born in these years tend to be quick-witted, clever and creative. They learn quickly and are good at solving problems. They can also be vain and selfish.

Years of the rooster: 1909, 1921, 1933, 1945, 1957, 1969, 1981, 1993. Those born in these years tend to be proud, upright and alert. They are also often precise and very direct. People born in these years also like to express themselves in speech, writing or music.

Years of the dog: 1910, 1922, 1934, 1946, 1958, 1970, 1982, 1994. Those born in these years are usually honest and loyal, straightforward and helpful. To them, fair play and justice are very important. A person born in these years will be a good friend to have.

Years of the pig (or boar): 1911, 1923, 1935, 1947, 1959, 1971, 1983, 1995. People born in these years are honest and straightforward. They can be relied on to see things through. They tend to be popular and make lasting friendships and are good neighbours.

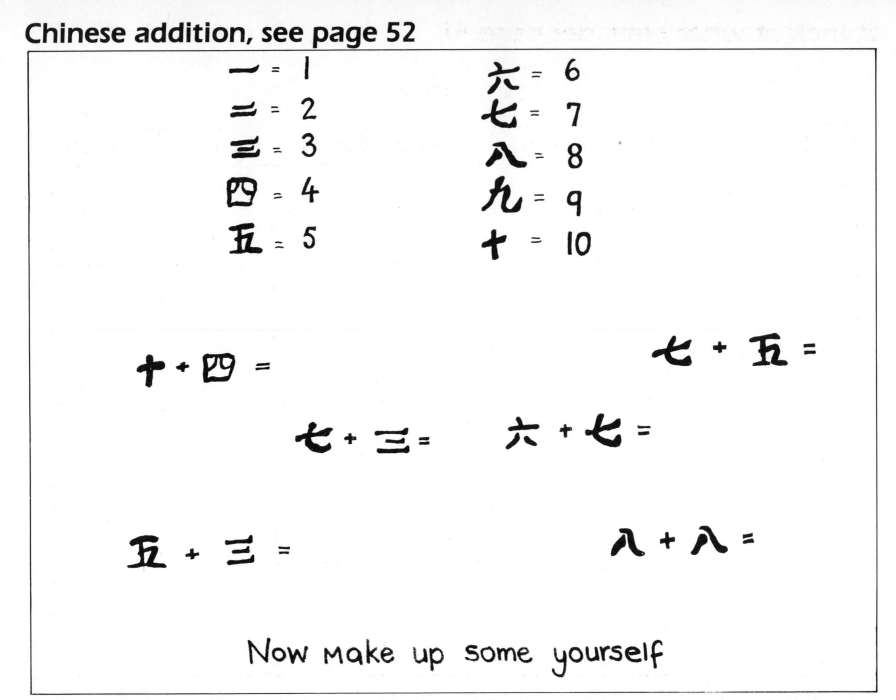

一 = 1

二 = 2

三 = 3

四 = 4

五 = 5

六 = 6

七 = 7

八 = 8

九 = 9

十 = 10

十 + 四 =

七 + 五 =

七 + 三 =

六 + 七 =

五 + 三 =

八 + 八 =

Now make up some yourself

A look at what I eat, see page 91

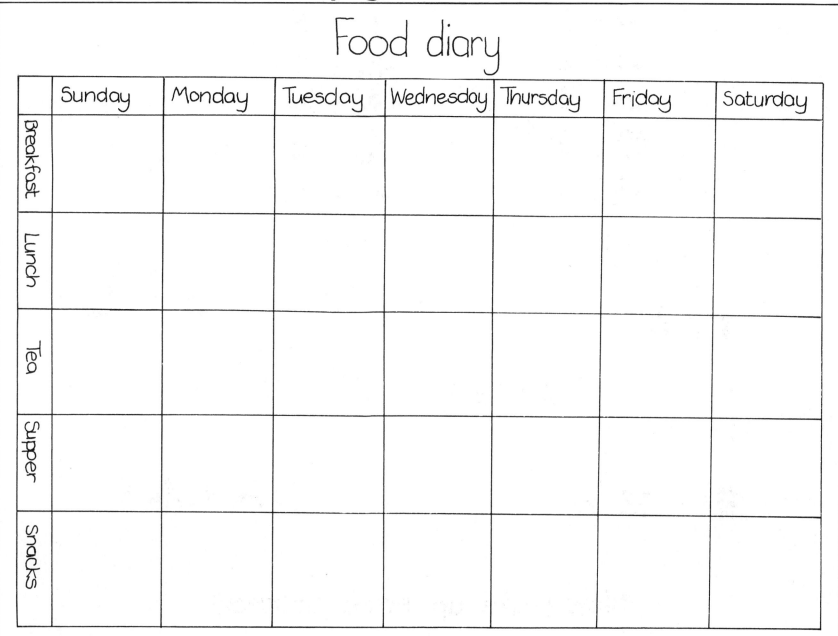

Food diary

	Sunday	Monday	Tuesday	Wednesday	Thursday	Friday	Saturday
Breakfast							
Lunch							
Tea							
Supper							
Snacks							

Other Scholastic books

Bright Ideas
The *Bright Ideas* books provide a wealth of resources for busy primary school teachers. There are now more than 20 titles published, providing clearly explained and illustrated ideas on topics ranging from *Writing* and *Maths Activities* to *Assemblies* and *Christmas Art and Craft*. Each book contains material which can be photocopied for use in the classroom.

Teacher Handbooks
The *Teacher Handbooks* give an overview of the latest research in primary education, and show how it can be put into practice in the classroom. Covering all the core areas of the curriculum, the *Teacher Handbooks* are indispensable to the new teacher as a source of information and useful to the experienced teacher as a quick reference guide.

Management Books
The *Management Books* are designed to help teachers to organise their time, classroom and teaching more efficiently. The books deal with topical issues, such as *Parents and Schools* and organising and planning *Project Teaching*, and are written by authors with lots of practical advice and experiences to share.

Let's Investigate
Let's Investigate is an exciting range of photocopiable activity books giving open-ended investigative tasks. Designed to cover the six to twelve-year-old age range, these books are ideal for small group or individual work. Each book presents progressively more difficult concepts and many of the activities can be adapted for use throughout the primary school. Detailed teacher's notes outlining the objectives of each photocopiable sheet and suggesting follow-up activities have been included.

Every effort has been made to trace and acknowledge contributors. If any right has been omitted, the publishers offer their apologies and will rectify this in subsequent editions following notification.